Report to Congress on Coordinating the American Opportunity Tax Credit and the Federal Pell Grant

U.S. DEPARTMENT OF THE TREASURY

May 5, 2014

The American Opportunity Tax Credit (AOTC), enacted as part of the American Recovery and Reinvestment Act, was signed by the President in February 2009. The same law mandated that a study be undertaken by the Secretary of the Treasury and the Secretary of Education, to examine 1) how to coordinate the AOTC with the Federal Pell Grant Program to maximize their effectiveness; 2) how to expedite delivery of the AOTC; and 3) whether it was feasible to require community service as a condition of eligibility for receiving the credit. This Treasury report on the findings of the study by the Department of Treasury and the Department of Education answers that mandate.

Executive Summary

The American Opportunity Tax Credit (AOTC), enacted as part of the American Recovery and Reinvestment Act (ARRA), was signed by the President in February 2009. The same law mandated that a study be undertaken by the Secretary of the Treasury and the Secretary of Education, or their delegates, to examine 1) how to coordinate the AOTC with the Federal Pell Grant Program to maximize their effectiveness; 2) how to expedite delivery of the AOTC; and 3) whether it was feasible to require community service as a condition of eligibility for receiving the AOTC.[1] The AOTC was extended to tax years 2011 and 2012 as part of the Tax Relief, Unemployment Insurance Reauthorization and Job Creation Act of 2010 (TRUIRJCA) and through 2017 as part of the American Tax Relief Act of 2012 (ATRA). The President's Fiscal Year 2014 (FY2014) Budget has called on Congress to make the AOTC permanent.

Summary of Findings:

1. **How to coordinate the AOTC with the Federal Pell Grant Program to maximize their effectiveness? Some options include:**

   * **Simplify the Financial Aid Formula and Remove the Asset Test**. In 2009, the Administration proposed legislation to simplify the formula for the Federal financial aid programs (including Pell Grants) by eliminating the question regarding contributions from savings and 14 other financial questions from the Free Application for Federal Student Aid (FAFSA). Removing these questions from the FAFSA would allow students to apply for aid using only the information found on their federal income tax forms. In combination with the current web-based IRS data retrieval tool, this option would make

---

[1] The statutory language appears in an appendix to this study.

the process of applying for and receiving Federal student aid much simpler, fairer, and more accurate. [2]

- **Create Web Estimates of AOTC Eligibility.** Under this option, students and their families would receive an estimate of their eligibility for an AOTC at the same time as they receive an estimate of their eligibility for Pell Grants and Federal loans. By showing the possibility of receiving an AOTC alongside the value of a Pell Grant, students would have a better sense of the total level of Federal aid that they could expect to receive.

- **Improve Information Reporting.** Under this option, information reporting on the Form 1098-T – which colleges and universities provide to the Internal Revenue Service as well as to students and their families – would be improved to ensure that eligible students are able to claim the full amount of benefits to which they are entitled and to ensure that claimants are in compliance with law.

- **Exclude Pell Grants from Taxable Income.** Under this option, a student's Pell Grant Award would be excluded from taxable income even if it is used for living expenses (current law permits an exclusion if the Pell Grant is used for tuition and fees). This option would allow more low-income students to claim the AOTC for tuition and use the Pell Grant for living expenses, increasing the amount of scholarship aid provided low-income students and making the calculation of the AOTC simpler.

2. **How to expedite delivery of the AOTC? Some options include:**

- **Making the AOTC Advance-Refundable**. This report considers the advantages and disadvantages of paying the AOTC in advance (that is, providing a refund of the tax

---

[2] In their study of the complexity of Federal student aid, Dynarski and Clayton (2006) find that assets have little impact on the calculation of federal aid. The authors simulated the effect of dropping the asset test from the FAFSA and found that without an asset test, 86 percent of Pell grants would have been within $500 of the grant received with the asset test in place.

credit prior to filing a tax return). The report finds that the limited advantages are outweighed by the disadvantages of this option. The report concludes that existing ways of delivering direct grant aid are better for delivering education subsidies in advance of tax filing to low-income students.

- **Integrate Delivery of the Refundable Portion of the AOTC into the Title IV Delivery System.** Under this option, an amount roughly equal to the refundable portion of the AOTC would be delivered to the student as a boost to their Pell Grant rather than as a refundable tax credit. The Pell Grant increase would be based on prior year tax data as provided on the FAFSA and would be administered by the Department of Education. A Pell "boost" would only be available for 4 years. The nonrefundable portion of the AOTC would not be changed. Alternatively, the savings from making the AOTC nonrefundable could be used to increase the Pell grant maximum award for all Pell recipients (however, some students would see the total amount of their Federal aid decline under this approach).

3. **Should Community Service Be a Condition of Eligibility for Receiving the AOTC?**

- **A Community Service Requirement Would Be Costly for the IRS and Higher Education Institutions to Administer and Might Not Serve Its Intended Purpose.** This report offers a framework for administering a volunteer requirement for AOTC eligibility and enumerates the challenges that would need to be overcome to implement such a requirement. The report concludes that while technically possible, such a requirement would be very costly for educational institutions and the IRS to administer.

I. Introduction

The American Recovery and Reinvestment Act of 2009 (ARRA) dramatically increased Federal support for higher education by increasing education tax credits and Pell Grants. ARRA created the American Opportunity Tax Credit (AOTC) as an enhancement and a replacement for the Hope credit. The AOTC is currently available through 2017. The AOTC provides a tax credit of up to $2,500 per student and up to $1,000 of this amount is refundable. ARRA also provided supplemental funding to Pell Grants to fund the estimated cost of the increase in the maximum award in 2010 to $5,550.

For tax year 2009, 9.0 million tax returns claimed $15.8 billion in American Opportunity Tax Credits for an average tax credit of about $1,760.[3] This level of education credits (including the lifetime learning credit) was over a $10 billion increase from the prior year. In addition, during FY2010 an estimated 8.9 million students received $36.5 billion in Pell Grant awards for an average award of $4,115.[4] As with the tax credits, the current funding levels represent a landmark increase in Federal support for college scholarships. Over the last decade, the number of Pell recipients has more than doubled and the total dollar amount of Pell Grants received has quadrupled.

While there is some coordination between the tax incentives and outlay programs, ARRA mandated a study to determine 1) if coordination could be improved; 2) if delivery of the credit could be expedited; and 3) if it is feasible to require community service as a condition of eligibility for the credit.[5,6] To answer this mandate, Section II of this report describes the higher education market, including who is currently going to school and at what cost; Section III describes current Federal support for higher education, both tax incentives and direct Federal student aid; Section IV describes the current level of coordination between Pell Grants and the

---

[3] Estimates reflect tax filings as of December 2010.

[4] U.S. Department of Education (2011), "FY 2012 Department of Education Justifications of Appropriation Estimates to the Congress: Student Financial Assistance" in *President's FY 2012 Budget Request for the U.S. Department of Education*, P-29.

[5] The statutory language appears in an appendix to this study.

[6] This study assumes throughout that "the credit" referenced in the statutory language is the AOTC. Section 25A also includes the lifetime learning credit but it was unchanged by ARRA.

AOTC, how the programs complement each other and where they are at odds; and Section V presents examples and graphs showing the level of tax credits and Pell Grants that a student could expect by type of institution and by income. The report generally reflects data from tax year 2009 and academic year 2009-10 and the education programs that were in place in 2009 and 2010. Section VI describes other coordination issues to consider; and Section VII discusses some options for increased coordination. Section VIII presents an option for expediting the delivery of the credit and Section IX discusses the feasibility of adding a service requirement as an additional condition of AOTC eligibility. Section X concludes.

II. Higher Education Market Overview

Table 1 documents changes in postsecondary enrollment over the last decade.[7] These data compare enrollments in the fall of 1999 to the fall of 2009. In the fall of 2009, 17.6 million undergraduate students were enrolled in a postsecondary institution, roughly 40 percent more than the number enrolled ten years earlier. Slightly more than 11 million students were enrolled full-time in the fall of 2009, an increase of 44 percent compared to the fall of 1999. Over 6 million students were enrolled part-time in 2009, compared to about 5 million part-time students in 1999. Although the number of part-time students increased substantially, due to the larger increase in full-time enrollments, this represents a 3.5 percent decrease in the share of students attending part-time. The distinction between full-time and part-time enrollment is important, because the amount of student aid for which a college-age person is eligible depends on enrollment intensity. For example, students enrolled less than half time are not eligible for the AOTC and students enrolled less than full time may not qualify as dependent children for purposes of the EITC or the dependency exemption.

The majority of both full-time and part-time students in both 1999 and in 2009 were enrolled in public institutions. Part-time enrollment increased between 1999 and 2009 for all school types except private not-for-profit 2-year schools, where enrollment contracted by 25 percent. Part-

---

[7] Table 1 does not include enrollments at less-than two-year institutions. The table is also limited to fall enrollments and may therefore understate total enrollments, particularly at two-year institutions.

time enrollment grew most rapidly at private for-profit institutions, increasing over 700 percent at 4-year schools and 62 percent at 2-year schools. Full-time enrollment also grew most rapidly at private for-profit schools, increasing over 400 percent at 4-year schools and over 100 percent at 2-year schools. Full-time enrollment increased between 1999 and 2009 for all other school types except private not-for-profit 2-year schools, where enrollment decreased by 50 percent.

Table 1
Number of Undergraduate Students by Part-Time Status and Institution Type,
Fall 2009 and Fall 1999

	Fall 2009 Enrollment		Fall 1999 Enrollment		Percent Change
	Thousand	Percent	Thousand	Percent	
Total Students	*17,565*	*100.0*	*12,681*	*100.0*	*38.5*
Total Part-Time	*6,422*	*36.6*	*4,946*	*39.0*	*29.8*
Private, for-profit 2-year	41	0.2	25	0.2	62.3
Private, for-profit 4-year	330	1.9	41	0.3	711.7
Private, not-for-profit 2-year	11	0.1	15	0.1	-25.3
Private, not-for-profit 4-year	439	2.5	416	3.3	5.6
Public 2-year	4,221	24.0	3,408	26.8	23.8
Public 4-year	1,381	7.9	1,042	8.2	32.5
Total Full-Time	*11,144*	*63.4*	*7,735*	*61.0*	*44.1*
Private, for-profit 2-year	345	2.0	166	1.3	107.6
Private, for-profit 4-year	871	5.0	157	1.2	454.5
Private, not-for-profit 2-year	23	0.1	47	0.4	-50.4
Private, not-for-profit 4-year	2,120	12.1	1,705	13.4	24.3
Public 2-year	2,881	16.4	1,931	15.2	49.2
Public 4-year	4,904	27.9	3,729	29.4	31.5

Source: Digest of Education Statistics: 2010, Table 202 and 2002 Table 178. National Center for Education Statistics, U.S. Department of Education.

Growth in enrollment across school types between 1999 and 2009 is reflected in changes in the number of institutions between these school years. Table 2 documents changes in the number of degree-granting institutions between the 1999-2000 academic year and the 2009-2010 academic year. As shown in this table the number of 4-year public and private not-for-profit schools has been relatively stable over the last 10 years. Compared to the 1999-2000 academic year, there were 9 percent more 4-year public schools and 1 percent more private not-for-profit 4-year schools in 2009-2010. In contrast, during this same period, the number of private not-for-profit

2-year schools dropped 43 percent, while the number of public 2-year schools decreased 6 percent. The number of private for-profit schools also grew substantially during this period. In the 1999-2000 school year, there were 721 private for-profit schools; by the 2009-2010 academic year, there were nearly 1,200 private for-profit schools.

Table 2
Total Number of Degree Granting Institutions,
2009-2010 and 1999-2000 Academic Years

	2009-2010	1999-2000	Percent Change
Private, for-profit 2-year	636	503	26.4
Private, for-profit 4-year	563	218	158.3
Private, not-for-profit 2-year	85	150	-43.3
Private, not-for-profit 4-year	1,539	1,531	0.5
Public 2-year	1,000	1,068	-6.4
Public 4-year	672	614	9.4

Note: Number of institutions includes branch campuses.
Source: Digest of Education Statistics: 2010, Table 275. National Center for Education Statistics, U.S. Department of Education.

The cost of an undergraduate education is substantial, and these costs are rapidly increasing. As shown in Table 3, during the 2009-2010 academic year, average published, as opposed to net after financial aid, tuition and required fees ranged from $2,300 at public 2-year institutions to $25,600 at 4-year private not-for-profit colleges and universities for full-time enrollees at degree-granting institutions. In comparison to prices ten years earlier, tuition and required fees had increased by 35 percent at 2-year public schools and by 20 percent at 2-year private not-for-profit institutions, adjusted for inflation. At 4-year institutions, tuition and required fees also increased, growing 36 percent at private not-for-profit institutions and 56 percent at public institutions (again, adjusted for inflation). Room and board charges increased substantially between the 1999-2000 and 2009-2010 academic years. Among 2-year institutions, room and board charges increased 9 percent at private not-for-profit institutions and 23 percent at public institutions (again, adjusted for inflation). Among 4-year schools, room and board charges increased 20 percent at private not-for-profit schools and 32 percent at public schools (again, adjusted for inflation).

7

Table 3

**Average Undergraduate Tuition and Room and Board,
2009-2010 and 1999-2000 Academic Years**

Institution Type	Tuition and Required Fees			Room and Board		
	2009-2010	1999-2000	Percent Change	2009-2010	1999-2000	Percent Change
Private, for-profit 2-year	15,100	-	-	10,900	-	-
Private, for-profit 4-year	15,200	-	-	10,100	-	-
Private, not-for-profit 2-year	12,700	10,600	19.8	8,100	7,400	9.5
Private, not-for-profit 4-year	25,600	18,800	36.2	9,500	7,900	20.3
Public 2-year	2,300	1,700	35.3	5,400	4,400	22.7
Public 4-year	6,700	4,300	55.8	8,300	6,300	31.7

Note: All dollar amounts in constant 2009 dollars and rounded to the nearest $100   Values for public institutions are charges for in-state students   Data not available for private, for-profit institutions in the 1999-2000 academic year

Source: Digest of Education Statistics: 2010, Table 345   National Center for Education Statistics, U S Department of Education

Table 4 shows graduation rates among full-time students who first enrolled in the fall of 2001.[8] The top panel of Table 4 shows graduation rates among those enrolled in 4-year institutions, and the bottom panel shows graduation rates for those enrolled in 2-year institutions. The majority of students enrolling as full-time students in public or private not-for-profit 4-year institutions completed their degree within six years. Among 4-year schools, students attending private not-for-profit institutions graduated at higher rates (64 percent) than students attending public institutions (55 percent). In contrast, only one in four students beginning at a private for-profit 4-year institution completed the degree within six years. Women who enrolled at 4-year schools were more likely than men to complete their bachelor's degree within six years at both public and private not-for-profit institutions although women were less likely to complete their degree at for-profit institutions. The majority of first-time college students who enrolled in a private not-for-profit or private for-profit 2-year institution in 2001 graduated with a certificate or associate's degree within 150 percent of normal time. Less than one in four first-time students who enrolled in a public 2-year school in 2001 completed their program within this time frame.

---

[8] Graduation rates are for students who are first-time, fall enrollees at students' initial institution.

Table 4
Graduation Rates of First-time Postsecondary Students Starting as
Full-time Degree Seeking Students in 2001, by Institution Type

	All Students	Male	Female
	Percent Completing Bachelor's Degree within 6 years after start		
Private, for-profit 4-year	25	28	21
Private, not-for-profit 4-year	64	61	67
Public 4-year	55	52	58
	Percent Completing Certificate or Associate's Degrees within 150 percent of normal time		
Private, for-profit 2-year	59	59	59
Private, not-for-profit 2-year	55	57	52
Public 2-year	23	22	24

Source: Digest of Education Statistics: 2009, Table 331. National Center for Education Statistics, U.S. Department of Education.

Table 5 shows the age distribution of students by institution type for students enrolled in the fall of 2009. Traditional college-age students (18-24) represented the majority of enrollment in most categories. At not-for-profit institutions and 2-year for-profit institutions, students aged 18-24 accounted for at least 47 percent of enrollment. By comparison, 4-year for-profit institutions enrolled relatively older students. In 2009, only 25 percent of all students enrolled at 4-year for-profit institutions were traditional college age. Many students in the 25-34 age range at 4-year institutions are likely to be graduate students or students seeking professional degrees. In contrast, students in this age range who attend 2-year institutions or for-profit institutions are likely working towards their first postsecondary degree. At 2-year public and 2-year private not-for-profit institutions, between 21 and 24 percent of students were between the ages of 25 and 34. At private for-profit institutions, students ages 25-34 accounted for 31 percent of enrollment at 2-year schools and 38 percent of enrollment at 4-year schools. Private for-profit 4-year institutions also enrolled a relatively larger share of students aged 35-49. This pattern suggests that private for-profit 4-year schools serve a different segment of the education market, compared to public and private not-for-profit institutions, or private for-profit 2-year schools.

Table 5
Share of Total Fall Enrollment by Student Age and Institution Type, 2009

	Under 24	25-34	35-49	50 and older
Private, for-profit 2-year	47	31	17	4
Private, for-profit 4-year	25	38	29	7
Private, not-for-profit 2-year	56	24	16	4
Private, not-for-profit 4-year	60	23	12	4
Public 2-year	60	21	14	5
Public 4-year	69	20	8	2

Notes: Enrollment at degree granting institutions, including both part-time and full-time students. For-profit enrollment calculated by author. Numbers do not add to 100 percent because age is unknown for some students.

Source: Digest of Education Statistics: 2010, Table 201. National Center for Education Statistics, U.S. Department of Education.

III. Overview of Federal Support for Higher Education

The American Opportunity Tax Credit and the Pell Grant are the largest federal provisions that support higher education but they are not the only provisions. In FY2010, over $145 billion of financial aid was available to undergraduate students in the form of federal grants, loans, and the Federal Work-Study Program (Federally subsidized jobs for students). In the same fiscal year, almost $29 billion in tax expenditures was also available to students and their families (see Table 6 below). In addition, states, colleges, universities, not-for-profit organizations, and the private sector also offer students financial assistance. During the 2009-2010 academic year, grant aid from these sources amounted to $41 billion.[9] Because interactions among the AOTC, Pell Grants, and the wider array of available programs affect the amount of aid available as a whole, this section briefly reviews all Federal support available to students pursuing higher education.

The wide array of programs is an attempt to address the needs of all students, for example those students who can only afford to attend part-time as well as those who attend full time, the young who are beginning their postsecondary educations, and older workers who need retraining. Some programs are designed to help parents save for future education expenses. Other programs

---

[9] See College Board (2010) Figure 2A.

10

support students currently in school, and still others alleviate the burden of repaying loans after schooling is complete.

A. Higher Education Tax Expenditures

Tax expenditures may take the form of a tax credit (refundable or non-refundable), a deduction, an exclusion, or a deferral. Generally, if an expense would qualify under more than one provision, current law allows only one tax benefit for the particular educational expense.

Table 6 shows estimates of the FY 2010 income tax expenditures for higher education.[10] Descriptions for each of the tax expenditures are provided below. At $15 billion, the tax expenditure estimate for the AOTC accounts for over half of all the higher education tax expenditures but there are other significant tax expenditures for higher education. The tax expenditure for the Lifetime Learning Credit, a credit targeted at older and less than half-time students, is $3.5 billion per year. The expenditure for the parental personal exemption for students age 19 and over is $3 billion annually and the annual tax expenditure for the exclusion of scholarship and fellowship income is $2.8 billion.

---

[10] Table 6 only shows the income tax expenditure for each provision. Provisions that exclude income may also affect a student or family's payroll tax liability. Tax expenditures are also calculated on a provision-by-provision basis. Although the total education related income tax expenditures amount to $29 billion per year, because of interaction affects repealing all of the tax expenditures listed in Table 6 would not be expected to raise $29 billion annually in revenue.

Table 6
Estimates of Higher Education Tax Expenditures for FY2010

	($ millions)
American Opportunity Tax Credit	$15,110
Lifetime Learning Tax Credit	$3,490
Parental personal exemption for students age 19 and over	$2,960
Exclusion of scholarship and fellowship income	$2,760
Deductibility of student-loan interest	$1,480
State prepaid tuition plans[1]	$1,390
Deduction for higher education expenses	$760
Exclusion of employer provided educational assistance	$680
Exclusion of interest on savings bonds	$20
Total	$28,650

Source: Table 17-2, *Fiscal Year 2012 Analytical Perspectives, Budget of the U.S. Government.*

[1] Includes tax expenditure for excluded earnings on all tax preferred education savings plans.

Tax Credits. In 1997, the *Hope Scholarship Credit* and the *Lifetime Learning Credit* (LLC) were created to help families with higher education expenses. In 2009, ARRA replaced the Hope Credit with the AOTC for tax years 2009 and 2010. TRUIRJCA extended the AOTC to tax years 2011 and 2012 and through 2017 as part of the ATRA. Prior to ARRA, a taxpayer could claim a Hope Credit for 100 percent of the first $1,200 and 50 percent of the next $1,200 in qualified tuition and related expenses (for a maximum credit of $1,800 per student) for the first two years of college for a student enrolled at least half-time. Qualified tuition and related expenses for the Hope credit was limited to tuition and fees required for enrollment or attendance of the taxpayer, the taxpayer's spouse or the taxpayer's claimed dependent. With the AOTC, a taxpayer can claim 100 percent of the first $2,000 and 25 percent of the next $2,000 in qualified tuition and related expenses (for a maximum credit of $2,500) for the first 4 years of college for a student enrolled at least half-time. Forty percent of the otherwise available AOTC is refundable (for a maximum refundable credit of $1,000). Qualified expenses under the AOTC were expanded to include required course materials, such as books.

Alternatively, a taxpayer may claim a nonrefundable LLC for 20 percent of up to $10,000 in qualified tuition and related expenses (for a maximum credit of $2,000) per taxpayer, irrespective of the number of students in the taxpayer's family, for any postsecondary education. Qualified expenses for the LLC only include tuition and fees required for enrollment or attendance, not course materials. In 2012, the LLC phased out for those earning between $52,000 and $62,000 of modified adjusted gross income (AGI) ($104,000 and $124,000 if married filing jointly) and the AOTC phased out between $80,000 and $90,000 of modified AGI ($160,000 and $180,000 if married filing jointly). Only one credit may be claimed by or on behalf of any eligible student.

Table 7 shows the distribution of returns that claimed an AOTC in 2009. In total, 9 million returns received $15.8 billion of AOTC in 2009 with an average AOTC of $1,760. Most returns with an AOTC had less than $150,000 of AGI. Upper middle-income returns tended to have slightly larger average credits than lower income returns because higher income families tend to have more eligible expenses. This is because, on average, they attend more expensive schools and are less likely to receive grant aid.

Table 7
American Opportunity Tax Credit - US Totals - Tax Year 2009

Adjusted Gross Income	Returns with AOTC					Dollars of AOTC					
	Total		Returns with Outlay			Total			Outlay		
	Thousands	Percent	Thousands	Percent	Percent with Outlay	$ Millions	Percent	Average	$ Millions	Percent	Average
Less than or Equal to $0	89	1 0	82	1 7	92 6	$81	0 5	$913	$73	1 9	$888
$0 to $10,000	990	11 0	977	20 1	98 7	$785	5 0	$793	$768	19 7	$786
$10,000 to $20,000	1,428	15 9	1,319	27 1	92 3	$1,517	9 6	$1,062	$1,031	26 5	$782
$20,000 to $30,000	1,150	12 8	979	20 2	85 1	$1,742	11 0	$1,515	$749	19 3	$765
$30,000 to $50,000	1,608	17 9	999	20 6	62 1	$3,018	19 1	$1,877	$821	21 1	$822
$50,000 to $75,000	1,281	14 3	396	8 1	30 9	$2,806	17 8	$2,191	$346	8 9	$874
$75,000 to $100,000	995	11 1	89	1 8	9 0	$2,355	14 9	$2,367	$87	2 2	$976
$100,000 to $150,000	1,115	12 4	17	0 3	1 5	$2,861	18 1	$2,565	$15	0 4	$909
$150,000 to $200,000	324	3 6	1	0 0	0 3	$637	4 0	$1,968	$0	0 0	$0
Over $200,000	0	0 0	0	0 0	0	$0	0 0	$0	$0	0 0	$0
Total	8,980	100 0	4,859	100 0	54 1	$15,802	100 0	$1,760	$3,890	100 0	$801

Notes: Excludes US Territories
    Taxpayers with negative AGI are not shown, but are included in the totals
Source: Statistics of Income (IRS), Individual Income Tax Returns for Tax Year 2009

As also shown in Table 7, 4.9 million returns received AOTC outlays in 2009 (outlays are the portions of the AOTC that are refunded). For these returns, the value of the AOTC that they received exceeded their individual income tax liability. This is the same population that is likely to be eligible for a Pell Grant.

The AOTC is partially but not fully refundable. Although the maximum AOTC is $2,500, if a taxpayer does not have $1,500 of tax liability then he or she cannot receive the maximum credit even if he or she would otherwise qualify because only $1,000 may be received as a refundable credit. A taxpayer with no individual income tax liability may receive a payment (referred to as an outlay or refundable credit) of up to a $1,000. Taxpayers with individual income tax liability greater than zero but less than $1,500 may receive a $1,000 outlay (refundable credit) plus a credit equal to their tax liability (if they are otherwise eligible). For example, if a taxpayer had $400 of tax liability before credits and otherwise qualified for a $2,500 AOTC, he or she would receive a $1,400 AOTC equal to a $1,000 refundable credit plus a $400 credit that would completely offset their individual income tax liability. Of the $15.8 billion dollars of AOTC in 2009, only $3.9 billion (25 percent) was an outlay. The average outlay was $801 in 2009.

Low-income working families may also be eligible for a (fully refundable) *earned income tax credit* (EITC). The value of the credit varies with the number of qualifying children, marital status, and with family income. In general, dependent children over the age of 18 do not qualify the taxpayer for this benefit. However, in the case of full-time students, the age limit is extended through 23. A married couple with one child would be eligible for an EITC of up to $3,169 in 2012, which would phase out completely at $42,130 of AGI.

Deductions. For parents supporting college students, there is also an extension of the benefit provided by the *dependency exemption deduction* for full-time students aged 19 through 23. Dependent children over the age of 18 do not qualify as children for the dependency exemption unless they remain full-time students (up to age 23). In 2012, the personal exemption amount was $3,800.

Taxpayers may also be eligible for a deduction above-the-line (i.e., without itemization) for up to $2,500 of interest per year on any qualified education loan, subject to a modified AGI phase-out between $60,000 and $75,000 ($120,000 and $150,000 if married filing jointly) in 2012.[11] The income tax expenditure for the deductibility of student-loan interest was $1.5 billion in FY2010.

Through tax year 2013, a taxpayer may also claim an above-the-line *deduction for qualified tuition and related expenses* (commonly referred to as the tuition deduction). The maximum amount of the deduction is $4,000 for taxpayers with AGI not exceeding $65,000 ($130,000 if married filing jointly), or $2,000 for taxpayers with AGI greater than $65,000 and not exceeding $80,000 (greater than $130,000 and not exceeding $160,000 if married filing jointly). The income tax expenditure for the deduction of higher education expenses was $800 million in FY2010.

In addition, deductions may be allowed for certain *work-related education expenses*. An employee who itemizes may deduct work-related education expenses as one of a class of miscellaneous itemized deductions subject to a floor of two percent of AGI.

An employee for whom the employer pays education expenses that would be deductible by the employee as work-related expenses if the employee had paid the expenses may exclude the amounts from gross income as a working condition fringe benefit.

Exclusions from Income. In addition to any available credits or deductions, a student who receives a *qualified scholarship* to a degree-granting program (including certain Federal medical training programs) may exclude from gross income amounts used to pay qualified tuition and related expenses, including fees, books, supplies, and required equipment. However, students must include in gross income the portion of scholarship awards and grants (including Pell Grants) that are used to pay living expenses. Under another provision, enacted in 1976 and substantially expanded in 1997 and 2007, a student may also exclude from gross income the amount of a loan that is forgiven if the student works for a required period of time in certain professions or locations. Additionally, there is an unlimited exclusion from the gift and

---

[11] ATRA made permanent the higher student loan interest deduction phase-out limits for joint filers (first enacted under EGTRRA). Modified AGI for the purpose of calculating the student loan interest deduction is AGI as calculated on a taxpayer's federal income tax return before subtracting any deduction for student loan interest.

generation-skipping transfer tax for tuition paid directly to a school on behalf of a student, resulting in an incentive to make gifts of college tuition for those donors (whether related or not to the student) who are living when the tuition payment is due.

There are also incentives for individuals to continue their education while employed. Since 1979, an employee has been allowed to exclude *employer-provided expenses* (up to $5,250 since 1986) that are part of an Educational Assistance Program (EAP).[12] Under an EAP, there is no requirement that the education be work-related. Employers may also exclude (without limit) from gross income employer reimbursements for work-related education spending made under a qualified accountable plan. To qualify as an accountable plan, the expenses must be work-related, the employee must adequately account to his or her employer for his or her expenses within a reasonable period of time, and the employee must return any reimbursement or allowance in excess of the expenses accounted for within a reasonable period of time. The tax expenditure for the exclusion of employer provided educational assistance was $700 million in FY2010.

Certain colleges and universities offer *tuition-reduction programs* to their employees (which can include the employee's spouse or dependent child). Tuition benefits under such programs may be excluded from gross income. Also, certain graduate students employed in teaching or research may exclude tuition reductions from gross income. As noted above, if an employer pays the educational expenses of an employee directly, the employee may exclude the payments from gross income as a working condition fringe benefit if the employee could have deducted the expenses as a work related educational expense had the employee paid the expense.

Savings Related Deferrals and Exclusions. Individuals may benefit from the deferral of tax by saving for retirement in an Individual Retirement Account (IRA). Withdrawals from IRAs made before the taxpayer is 59½ are generally subject to a 10 percent additional income tax (in addition to the ordinary income tax on taxable distributions). Since 1997, an IRA distribution for qualified higher education expenses has been permitted, with the 10 percent additional income

---

[12] The employer provided education provision has been extended repeatedly, most recently by ATRA which made it permanent.

tax waived, although the ordinary income tax on the taxable portion of the distribution is still due. The exemption from the additional income tax covers both Traditional and Roth IRAs, allowing for tax-deferred saving effectively without income limits on contributors, encompassing family members including grandchildren as beneficiaries, and extending beyond tuition and fees to room and board (for students attending college at least half-time).

In addition, individuals at all income levels may contribute to *Qualified Tuition Programs*, or section 529 plans. These plans can take the form of a 529 savings account or a prepaid tuition plan. In either case, contributions accumulate tax free and are not taxed upon distribution if used for qualified education expenses. The plans are run by the States, with the exception of one plan that provides a prepaid tuition plan for a consortium of private postsecondary institutions. Some states also permit contributors to deduct a limited amount of contributions for state income tax purposes. The tax expenditure for the exclusion of earnings accruing in all prepaid tuition and savings plans was $1.4 billion in FY2010.

In 1997, an additional tax preferred savings vehicle was created in the form of an *Education IRA*. Subject to an AGI phase-out, contributors were allowed to contribute up to $500 per beneficiary per year to an Education IRA. The contribution limit was increased in 2001 to $2,000 for each beneficiary and the accounts were renamed Coverdell Education Savings Accounts (ESAs). Like 529s, contributions to Coverdell ESAs accumulate tax free and are not taxed upon distribution if used for qualified expenses.

Finally, subject to income limitations, an exclusion from income of interest on qualified United States Savings Bonds has been available since 1988, provided that the proceeds are used to pay for qualified higher education expenses. The tax expenditure for the exclusion of interest on savings bonds was $20 million in FY2010.

B. Direct Federal Financial Aid for College Students

The principal Federal student financial assistance programs are authorized under Title IV of the Higher Education Act of 1965, as amended, and provide grant, loan and work-study assistance to students and their families.

Table 8 shows the amount of Federal aid available by program. The major programs are described briefly below. Pell Grants and Federal loans are the largest programs.

	Amount ($ millions)	Recipients (thousands)	Average ($)
Table 8			
Federal Postsecondary Student Aid FY2010			
Pell Grants	$36,515	8,873	$4,115
Supplemental Educational Opportunity Grants	$959	1,339	$716
Federal Work-Study	$1,171	713	$1,642
Leveraging Educational Assistance Partnerships	$162	162	$1,000
Academic Competitiveness Grants	$548	786	$697
SMART Grants	$384	150	$2,500
Federal Family Education Loans[1,2]	$19,618	5,220	$3,758
Federal Direct Loans[2]	$84,704	16,646	$5,089
Perkins Loans	$971	493	$1,968
TEACH Grants	$109	37	$2,966
Iraq and Afghanistan Service Grants	*	*	$4,816
Subtotal Student Loans	$105,400		
Total[3]	$145,138		

* Less than $1 million or 1,000 recipients.

[1] This program ended June 30, 2010, as stipulated in the Student Aid and Fiscal Responsibility Act. All new loans as of July 1, 2010 are originated in the Federal Direct Loan Program.
[2] Loan amounts reflect the face value of the loan, not the subsidy level.

[3] Totals may not sum due to rounding.

Source: Fiscal Year 2013 Budget Department of Education

Need-Based Grants. Pell Grants are need-based grants available to low-income undergraduate students.[13] They are the largest source of grant aid and are available for use at more than 5,400

---

[13] Certain post-baccalaureate students in teacher certification programs may also be eligible.

institutions with more than 1 in 3 undergraduates receiving a Pell award during the 2010-2011 award year.[14] Recipients must be undergraduates and cannot have received a bachelor's degree previously (with the exception of certain teacher certificate programs), and must be enrolled with the purpose of obtaining a degree or certificate at an eligible institution. Students must have a high school diploma (or its equivalent). Less than full-time students are eligible for pro rata awards based on their enrollment status.

As shown in Table 8, in FY2010, the Pell Grant program offered $36.5 billion in aid to more than 8.8 million undergraduate students for an average grant of $4,115.[15] In contrast, in FY2008 the Pell program offered half as much aid, $18.3 billion to 6.2 million students for an average grant of $2,971.[16]

There are four major causes behind the growth in Pell Grant costs:

1. Demographic changes and increases in the number of eligible students (40 percent of increase). The largest single driver of Pell Grant cost increases has been the increase in applicants and their relative financial need. Because of the recent recession, more individuals chose to pursue or return to higher education and a higher percentage of students were from low-income families. The largest growth in applicants has been among those in the lowest income categories who receive the largest Pell Grants.

2. Increases to the maximum award (22 percent of increase). Between 2008 and 2009, the discretionary maximum Pell Grant grew by $619, from $4,241 to $4,860. Additional (mandatory) funding increased the maximum Pell by another $690 to $5,550.

---

[14] See Department of Education, "Description of Federal Pell Grant Program," http://www2.ed.gov/programs/fpg/index.html, "Postsecondary Institutions and Price of Attendance in 2011-2012, Degrees and Other Awards Conferred: 2010-2011, and 12-Month Enrollment: 2010-2011 First Look Provisional Data," http://nces.ed.gov/pubs2012/2012289rev.pdf, and "Title IV Program Volume Reports" http://studentaid.ed.gov/about/data-center/student/title-iv.
[15] U.S. Department of Education (2011) "FY 2012 Department of Education Justifications of Appropriation Estimates to the Congress: Student Financial Assistance" in *President's FY 2012 Budget Request for the U.S. Department of Education*, P-24.
[16] Ibid.

3. Second Pell/Year-round Pell (21 percent of the increase). The Higher Education Opportunity Act of 2008 created "year-round Pell Grants," which allowed students who complete more than two semesters of study in one school year to receive an additional (i.e., second) Pell Grant for a summer semester. This benefit was originally projected to cost about $300 million a year but take-up was much higher than anticipated. Approximately 10 percent of Pell recipients benefitted in 2010 creating costs more than ten times higher than the Congressional Budget Office's original estimate.[17]

4. Need analysis changes (14 percent of the increase). Legislation in 2007 and 2008 expanded the number of students who qualify for the maximum award, and allowed some students to qualify for larger awards. These need analysis changes were generally targeted at the neediest students.[18]

Table 9 shows the distribution of Pell Grant recipients and awards by income for the 2009-2010 academic year. Pell Grants are generally awarded to dependent students whose parents have income less than $60,000 per year and to independent students whose income is less than $30,000 per year.[19] Grant amounts are calculated using a formula that compares costs of attendance to the expected contribution of the student and his or her family to the student's education (the Expected Family Contribution, or EFC) with any shortfall made up by a Pell Grant, subject to the maximum award amount for that year. The cost of attendance includes tuition and fees, books, and living expenses. The EFC is calculated by the Department of Education using a statutory formula that considers the financial resources and household

---

[17] This benefit was eliminated by Congress after 2011.

[18] Over the past several years, Congress and the Administration have enacted a series of changes to student aid programs to provide sufficient budget authority to fund the maximum award. The 2011 Appropriation bill eliminated the availability of two full Pell awards in an academic year. The Budget Control Act eliminated graduate students' eligibility for subsidized loans and appropriated the savings to the Pell Grant program. In the Consolidated Appropriations Act of 2012, additional changes were made to the Federal student aid programs to ensure that there were sufficient resources to pay for the $5,550 maximum Pell Grant. The changes included raising the minimum award level to 10 percent, eliminating the interest subsidy on subsidized Stafford loans during the grace period for academic years 2012-2013 and 2013-2014, decreasing the maximum eligibility for Pell Grants from 18 to 12 semesters, reducing the income threshold for an automatic maximum grant, and tightening eligibility rules to exclude new students without a high school diploma or the equivalent. The changes became effective July 1, 2012.

[19] The income limits described here assume a very simple case where families have few other resources and very limited assets. The actual process for determining eligibility is complex and various financial factors will affect these cut-offs.

circumstances of the student and the student's family (including, primarily, the student's income and financial assets, the family's income and financial assets, family size, and the number of additional family members attending postsecondary education). Part-time students and students attending less than a full academic year receive prorated grants. Notably, although private for-profit institutions account for 9 percent of enrollments, they accounted for over 25 percent of total Pell Grant recipients in 2009-2010.

Table 9
Distribution of Pell Grant Recipients and Awards by Income for Academic Year 2009-2010

Total Income[1]	Pell Grant Recipients		Pell Grant Awards		
	Thousands	Percent	Total $ Millions	Percent	Average
Less than or Equal to $0	800	9.9	$3,181	10.6	$3,975
$0 to $10,000	1,956	24.2	$7,976	26.6	$4,078
$10,000 to $20,000	2,006	24.8	$7,512	25.0	$3,744
$20,000 to $30,000	1,361	16.8	$5,653	18.8	$4,154
$30,000 to $50,000	1,519	18.8	$4,762	15.9	$3,136
$50,000 to $75,000	432	5.3	$872	2.9	$2,019
$75,000 to $100,000	19	0.2	$33	0.1	$1,740
$100,000 to $150,000	1	0.0	$3	0.0	$3,361
$150,000 to $200,000	0	0.0	$0	0.0	
Over $200,000	0	0.0	$0	0.0	
Total	8,094	100.0	$29,992	100.0	$3,706

[1] Income is measured at 2008 levels. Total Income equals AGI plus untaxed income and benefits.

Source: Unpublished tabulations from the U.S. Department of Education.

In addition to Pell Grants, *Federal Supplemental Educational Opportunity Grants* (FSEOGs) are available to undergraduates with exceptional financial need. Like Federal Work-Study and Perkins Loan, FSEOG is a campus-based program. Institutions select FSEOG recipients and set their grant levels, but Federal guidelines stipulate that students with "exceptional need" and who are Pell Grant recipients have priority in the selection process. Thus, the financial aid office at a student's school has some discretion over who receives an FSEOG and how much they receive. Schools that choose to participate in the FSEOG program must contribute one dollar for every three dollars they receive from the Federal government. Approximately 3,800 schools participated in the FSEOG program in FY2010. The maximum FSEOG is $4,000 a year.

Approximately 1.3 million students received $959 million in FSEOG awards in FY2010 for an average award of $716.

Other Grant Programs. The *Academic Competitiveness Grant* (ACG) was made available for the first time for the 2006-2007 academic year. It provided up to $750 for the first year of undergraduate study to students who had completed a rigorous secondary school program and up to $1,300 for the second year of undergraduate study to students who maintained at least a cumulative 3.0 grade point average (GPA) on a 4.0 scale as of the end of the first year of undergraduate study. The ACG award was restricted to Pell recipients and was in addition to the student's Pell Grant award. Approximately 786,000 students received $548 million in ACG grants in FY2010 for an average award of almost $700.[20]

The *National Science & Mathematics Access to Retain Talent Grant* (National SMART Grant) provided up to $4,000 per academic year during the third and fourth years of undergraduate study (or fifth year of a five-year program) to at least half-time students who were eligible for the Federal Pell Grant and who were majoring in physical, life, or computer sciences, mathematics, technology, engineering or a critical foreign language; or non-major single liberal arts programs. The student was also required to maintain a cumulative grade point average (GPA) of at least 3.0 in course work required for the major. The National SMART Grant award was in addition to the student's Pell Grant award. Approximately 150,000 students received $384 million in SMART grants in FY2010 for an average award of $2,500.[21]

The *TEACH Grant* Program was created in the College Cost Reduction and Access Act of 2007. It provides up to $4,000 per year to students who intend to teach in a public or private elementary or secondary school that serves students from low-income families. (Students who fail to complete the teaching requirement must repay the grant with interest in the form of an unsubsidized Stafford loan.)

---

[20] Funding authority for ACG program expired on June 30, 2011.
[21] Authority to make National SMART grants ended June 30, 2011.

Loans.[22] A _Federal Perkins Loan_ is a low-interest loan for both undergraduate and graduate students with exceptional financial need. Eligible students may borrow up to $5,500 for each year of undergraduate study (maximum of $27,500 for undergraduate study) and up to $8,000 per year for graduate study (maximum of $60,000 for both undergraduate and graduate study). Students do not pay interest on the loan while in school or during nine month grace period after leaving school. Approximately 500,000 students received almost $971 million in Perkins loans in FY2010 with an average loan of $1,968.[23]

A _Direct Subsidized Stafford Loan_[24] is a low interest rate loan available to students with financial need. The maximum amount a student may borrow in the first undergraduate year is $3,500 but the yearly maximum increases with succeeding years of schooling. Students whose loans originated prior to July 1, 2012 do not pay interest on the loan while in school or during six month grace period after leaving school.

A _Direct Unsubsidized Stafford Loan_ is a low interest rate loan available to all students independent of need. The maximum amount a student may borrow is $5,500 (including the amount of any subsidized loan) in the first undergraduate year but the yearly maximum increases with succeeding years of schooling. Interest on the loan accrues from the time of disbursement but payment may be deferred while the student is in school and during the six month grace period after leaving school.

C. State and Institutional Aid

As shown in Table 10, 64 percent of full-time, full-year students receive grant aid, 33 percent receive Federal grant aid and 53 percent receive state, institutional and/or private grants (some

---

[22] The loan programs described here are those available in 2009 and 2010. The rules and limits for currently available loans may differ from those described in this report.

[23] Statutory authority to operate the Perkins loan program will expire in 2014.

[24] Before July 1, 2010, Stafford, PLUS, and Consolidation Loans were also made by private lenders under the Federal Family Education Loan (FFEL) Program. As a result of recent legislation, no further loans are being made under the FFEL Program beginning July 1, 2010. All new Stafford, PLUS, and Consolidation Loans will come directly from the Department under the Direct Loan Program.

students receive both Federal and state grant aid). Only 36 percent of full-time, full-year students paid the published tuition and fees (or "sticker price") for their schooling.

As also shown in Table 10, students receive substantial amounts of grant aid. For example, average published tuition and fees (excluding room and board) at a 4-year public school was $6,191 in 2007-2008 but the average *non-Federal* grant award (including awards for room and board) for a student receiving an award was $5,170. There are two potential interactions of federal and non-federal aid to note. First, additional aid by the Federal government may be offset or redirected at the institutional level. Because many institutions try to meet the financial need of their admitted students, if a student's Federal grant aid increases by $100, the institution may decrease that student's institutional grant aid by $100 or some portion of $100 and redirect the money toward other uses – such as merit aid, lower tuition, or enhanced facilities. Second, because institutional aid is significant it may decrease the amount a student may be able to claim for an AOTC.

Table 10										
Percent of Full-Time, Full-Year Undergraduate Students Receiving Aid and Average Amount Received 2007-2008 by Source and Institution Type										
Institution Type	**Any Aid**			**Grants**			**Loans**			**Federal Work Study**
	Total	Federal	Other	Total	Federal	Other	Total	Federal	Other	
All Institutions	79.5	63.0	62.9	64.4	33.0	52.8	53.3	49.6	20.1	10.3
Private, not-for-profit	89 1	70 0	81 8	80 6	28 3	76 0	64 9	60 9	29 1	23 7
Public 4-year	76 7	57 5	62 1	58 9	26 1	53 1	52 7	48 6	17 1	8 4
Public 2-year	65 4	49 2	46 6	53 9	35 1	40 4	24 8	21 5	7 8	
Private, for-profit	96 9	93 6	60 1	72 3	62 2	25 4	92 0	88 7	44 0	1 8
All Institutions	$12,740	$8,070	$8,020	$7,110	$3,670	$6,390	$9,480	$7,050	$7,780	$2,160
Private, not-for-profit	$20,740	$9,660	$14,310	$12,070	$4,060	$11,300	$12,160	$8,220	$9,910	$1,920
Public 4-year	$11,470	$8,220	$6,560	$6,340	$3,700	$5,170	$8,880	$7,080	$7,220	$2,310
Public 2-year	$5,650	$5,130	$2,520	$3,660	$3,270	$1,850	$5,450	$4,600	$4,690	$2,790
Private, for-profit	$13,120	$9,270	$6,700	$3,990	$3,280	$3,300	$10,260	$7,110	$7,140	$3,700

Note: Aid averages are for those students who received the specified type of aid Full-time, full-year students are defined as enrolled full-time for 9 or more months from July 1 through June 30

Source: U S Department of Education, National Center for Education Statistics, *2007-08 National Postsecondary Student Aid Studies*, Tables 343 and 344

IV. Comparing the American Opportunity Tax Credit and Pell Grant

Pell Grants and the AOTC make college more affordable for undergraduate students and their families. They target aid to needy families who are burdened by the high (and rising) cost of a postsecondary education. The Pell Grant is targeted to the neediest families; over half of Pell Grants are received by families with less than $20,000 of income. The AOTC provides tax relief to middle-income families as well as refundable credits for low-income families.

The AOTC is calculated as 100 percent of the first $2,000 and 25 percent of the next $2,000 in expenses for qualified tuition, fees and course materials (for a maximum credit of $2,500) for the first 4 years of college for a student enrolled at least half-time. The Pell Grant is calculated as the difference between a student's Expected Family Contribution (EFC) and the cost of attendance including room and board up to a maximum grant of $5,550 in 2012. The EFC is calculated as a function of parental income, student income, and other characteristics affecting available resources. Pell Grants are taxable to the extent that they are used to pay living expenses,[25] and like all other scholarship income, are considered earned income to the student. Only amounts used to pay tuition and other eligible expenses such as required fees and books are excludable from gross income.

Higher education institutions are involved in the administration of Pell Grants and, to a limited extent, the verification of student eligibility for the AOTC. Students apply for and are awarded a grant through the Free Application for Federal Student Aid. Once a grant amount is determined by the EFC, the student can use the grant at any institution. However, the Pell Grant is not disbursed directly to the student, but rather to the school. The schools apply the Pell Grant received by a student to his or her eligible school expenses and disburse remaining funds (if any) to the student to pay other eligible expenses directly. As discussed below, Pell Grants have a more expansive list of eligible expenses than the AOTC.

---

[25] Stipends to recipients for participants in the National Health Service Corps Scholarship Program and the Armed Forces Health Professions Scholarship Program are excluded from income.

All higher education institutions eligible to participate in the Department of Education's student aid programs are required to file an information return, Form 1098-T, with the IRS for all enrolled students (with a few exceptions).[26] A copy of the 1098-T return is also sent to the student. As shown in Figure 1, the 1098-T records either payments received for tuition and related expenses required for enrollment (Box 1) or amounts billed for tuition and related expenses (Box 2). It is up to each school whether to fill in Box 1 or Box 2. The amounts recorded in either box only include tuition and fees required for enrollment and include scholarships and grants administered by the institution for the student. The scholarships and grants administered by the school are recorded in Box 5. Such amounts include all Federal and institutional grants but exclude private grants that are not administered by the school. The 1098-T also includes a check-box to indicate that the student is enrolled at least half-time (Box 8) and a check-box to indicate that the student is enrolled as a graduate student (Box 9).

Figure 1

8383 ☐ VOID ☐ CORRECTED

FILER'S name, street address, city, state, ZIP code, and telephone number		1 Payments received for qualified tuition and related expenses $ 2 Amounts billed for qualified tuition and related expenses $	OMB No. 1545-1574 **2011** Form **1098-T**	**Tuition Statement**
FILER'S federal identification no.	STUDENT'S social security number	3 Check if you have changed your reporting method for 2011 ☐		**Copy A For Internal Revenue Service Center** File with Form 1096. For Privacy Act and Paperwork Reduction Act Notice, see the **2011 General Instructions for Certain Information Returns.**
STUDENT'S name		4 Adjustments made for a prior year $	5 Scholarships or grants $	
Street address (including apt. no.) City, state, and ZIP code		6 Adjustments to scholarships or grants for a prior year $	7 Check this box if the amount in box 1 or 2 includes amounts for an academic period beginning January - March 2012 ► ☐	
Service Provider/Acct. No. (see instr.)	8 Check if at least half-time student ☐	9 Check if a graduate student . . . ☐	10 Ins. contract reimb./refund $	

Form **1098-T** Cat. No. 25087J Department of the Treasury - Internal Revenue Service

Do Not Cut or Separate Forms on This Page — Do Not Cut or Separate Forms on This Page

[26] There are a few filing exceptions for the 1098-T. Schools do not have to file a 1098-T for: courses for which no academic credit is offered, even if the student is otherwise enrolled in a degree program; non-resident alien students, unless requested by the student; students whose qualified tuition and related expenses are entirely waived or paid entirely with scholarships; and students for whose qualified tuition and related expenses are covered by a formal billing arrangement where the institution bills only the student's employer or a government entity and does not maintain a separate financial account for the student.

Thus the 1098-T provides third-party verification that the student is enrolled at an eligible institution and indicates whether the student is enrolled at least half time, and whether the student is a graduate or undergraduate student. Only students who attend an eligible institution at least half-time and who pay tuition and related expenses out-of-pocket are eligible for an AOTC. Unfortunately, as discussed below (Section VI), the expense and grant information provided on the Form 1098-T is not sufficient to verify that a student's expenses are eligible for the AOTC. This omission makes it more difficult for the student (or the student's family) to calculate expenses eligible for the AOTC and more difficult for the IRS to verify compliance.

The following describes other similarities and differences between the Pell Grant Program and the AOTC.

A. Similarities

Undergraduate students only: Both the Pell Grant and the AOTC are generally limited to undergraduate students.[27]

Part-time students: Both Pell Grants and the AOTC are available to less than full-time students. Pell Grants are available to students at any level of participation as long as they have not completed their first bachelor's degree. Grants are prorated for part-time students. The AOTC is available to students attending half-time or more.

Income limitations: Neither Pell Grants nor the AOTC are available to very high income families. Pell Grants are generally restricted to families with less than $60,000 of income. The AOTC is restricted to taxpayers with less than $90,000 of modified AGI ($180,000 if married filing jointly).

---

[27] With the exception noted above that in some cases, students who are enrolled in teacher training programs after completing a bachelor's degree may still be eligible for a Pell Grant. Also, graduate students who have not completed four years of postsecondary programs may be eligible for the AOTC. A taxpayer may claim the AOTC only for four taxable years for each eligible student.

Low-income families: Both Pell Grants and the AOTC are available to very low-income families. Up to $1,000 of the AOTC is refundable, meaning that it is available to families who have no income tax liability. As shown in Table 9 above (Section III), over half of students with Pell Grants have family incomes of less than $20,000 and as shown in Table 7 above, over half of the taxpayers receiving an AOTC receive a credit that exceeds their income tax liability.

Eligibility based on tax data: Both Pell Grants and the AOTC use tax data to determine eligibility. Because Pell Grants use income data from the prior tax year, eligibility for Pell Grants can be determined earlier and the grant made available at the start of the school term. Pell Grants also use asset information for the student and parent(s) although, as discussed below (Section VII), the additional information may not greatly affect eligibility.

B. Differences

In general Pell Grants are designed to target aid to the lowest income students; whereas, the AOTC offers targeted tax relief to low- and middle-income students and their families. The average Pell Grant ($4,115) is much larger than the average AOTC ($1,730). Pell Grants are paid directly to the school at the time tuition is due and may form the foundation of an aid package (including a family's expected contribution) designed to cover both tuition and living expenses. In contrast, the AOTC offers tax relief to taxpayers who incurred out-of-pocket expenses for tuition, fees or course materials (including books) with the credit being claimed when the tax return is filed (generally months after tuition costs are incurred).

Determination of need: As discussed previously, Pell Grants are generally restricted to families with less than $60,000 of income and the AOTC is restricted to taxpayers with less than $90,000 of modified AGI ($180,000 if married filing jointly). Specifically, however, the determination of need for Pell Grants is dependent on many factors. Under the Department of Education's need analysis formulas, a family's eligibility varies with family size, the number of students in the family attending college, whether the student is a dependent or not (see below), the financial assets of the student, and in the case of a dependent student, the income and financial assets of the parent(s). Under the AOTC, the computation of need is only dependent on modified AGI and filing status. One option to coordinate the credits (Option 1 Section VII) would limit the information used to determine Pell Grant eligibility to data available on a tax return. Such a change would make the assessment of need between the Pell and the AOTC similar, although the income limitations for the AOTC would remain higher.

Definition of dependent: Unmarried students aged 19 to 23 who provide for their own support are not treated as their parent's dependents under the tax code but are treated as dependents of their parents under the financial aid rules for the Pell Grant. Under Federal financial aid formulas, unmarried students younger than 24 are generally considered to be dependents, and their families are generally expected to contribute to their education. Pell Grant awards are based on this expectation and therefore may be lower or denied if the parents have significant income, even in the case where the parents do not actually contribute to the child's education.[28] The age limitation is intended to limit the receipt of aid to those students who do not have access to parental resources.

For purposes of the dependency exemption deduction, to qualify as a dependent, a child must be younger than 19 years old, or younger than 24 years old and a full-time student, and who does not provide more than half of his or her own support.[29] For purposes of the AOTC, if a student is a claimed dependent of another taxpayer, only that taxpayer may claim the AOTC for that student. However, if another taxpayer is eligible but does not claim the student as a dependent, then only the student can claim the AOTC.[30]

---

[28] For the most part independent students, as defined by Federal financial aid regulations, have attained their 24th birthday. Younger students can qualify as independent if they have children, are married, are veterans of the Armed Forces, are graduate students, or if their parents are deceased. These types of students are treated the same as older independent students for purposes of Federal financial aid.

[29] The rules described here that relate to the tax codes definition of dependency are an overview. The other conditions that must be met for dependency are that the child must have lived with the taxpayer for more than half of the year (living at school qualifies), and the child must not file a joint return for the year unless it is being filed solely for the purpose of claiming a refund. More detailed rules may apply to specific situations (e.g. permanently disabled children are not subject to age tests). See IRS publication 501 for a complete list of rules at http://www.irs.gov/pub/irs-pdf/p501.pdf.

[30] Payments of tuition, required fees and books by third parties (including parents) are deemed to be expenses paid by the student for the purposes of claiming the education tax credits. However, payment of these expenses by a parent is treated as support paid by the parent for the determination of dependency for tax purposes.

Tax Liability Limitation: The level of a Pell Grant is determined by a student's need and is only limited by the amount of qualifying expenses and by enrollment intensity (part-time students receive smaller awards). Similar to the Pell Grant, the AOTC is directed at needy families (the credit is phased out with income) and is limited to eligible expenses (albeit a narrower definition of eligible expenses, see below). The AOTC is also limited by a taxpayer's individual income tax liability. For example, if a taxpayer has no individual income tax liability, then the maximum AOTC is only $1,000. In all cases, the refundable portion of the AOTC is limited to $1,000.

Qualifying Expenses: Pell Grants can be used to pay for tuition, required fees, book, *and* living expenses such as room and board and childcare. Eligible expenses for the AOTC include only tuition, required fees, and course materials (including books) paid in the tax year for an academic period that begins in the same tax year or the first 3 months of the following tax year.

Years of eligibility: A student may receive a Pell Grant for up to 12 semesters (or its equivalent) provided that the student is still pursuing his or her first bachelor's degree. In contrast, the AOTC is only available for the first four years of undergraduate postsecondary education. A taxpayer may claim the AOTC only for four taxable years for each eligible student.

The lifetime learning credit and tuition deduction are available for students pursuing any postsecondary education and are available for any taxable year.

Timing of disbursements: Pell Grants are generally disbursed once per term (semester, trimester, or quarter) by the school. The school may apply the Pell Grant award to school costs or pay the student directly. In either case, the Pell Grant award is available at the time tuition is due. In contrast, absent changes to withholding in the case of students receiving nonrefundable credits and in all cases for a student receiving refundable credits, an AOTC is only received after the taxpayer has filed his or her tax return. For expenses paid in 2012, a taxpayer would receive the credit in 2013 (usually by the April 15th filing deadline). For students that do not have the means to finance the tuition payment when it is due, the AOTC would have little value as a way to pay for schooling in the first year. In subsequent years, the AOTC could be saved for future tuition bills. The timing of the delivery of grant and other financial aid (including loans) generally serves the neediest students best.

V. Examples and Graphs of the Interaction between Pell Grants and the AOTC

A. Examples of Interaction

Tables 11 and 12 show examples of how the Pell Grant and the AOTC interact using two levels of taxpayer income and 3 levels of tuition, required fees and books. Table 11 shows examples where the student is the claimed child dependent of a head of household filer who pays the expenses. The examples show the tax liability for the entire family, including (potential) tax liability faced by the student due to receipt of the Pell Grant. Table 12 continues with Examples 7, 8, and 9. In this table, the student is a head of household filer who has one young dependent child. In this case, the Pell Grant is income to the taxpayer and affects the taxpayer's liability. In both tables all income, with the exception of any scholarship income, is from wages. These examples illustrate how the grant may be allocated to maximize the family's tax benefits. All the examples in Table 11 and 12 assume that the family optimizes its total tax and grant benefits. Boxes 1 and 2 at the end of this subsection, give examples of how much a family might lose if they do not optimize.

In order to optimize its benefits, the family must decide whether to use its grant to pay for room and board (or other eligible living expenses), use it to pay tuition, required fees, and books (AOTC eligible expenses), or a combination. If a family uses some or all of its grant to pay AOTC eligible expenses then that portion of the grant must be subtracted from expenses eligible for an AOTC. If a family uses some or all of its grant to pay room and board or other living expenses, then that portion of the grant must be included in the income of the student for tax purposes. In most of the Table 11 examples the income of the dependent student remains below the filing threshold for dependent filers ($5,800 for dependent filers with only earned income) and no tax will be owed.

Families optimize their tax benefits by first using scholarships (including Pell Grants) to pay AOTC eligible expenses in excess of $4,000. If a family still has $4,000 or more of expenses for tuition, required fees and books after using its scholarships to pay these expenses, then it will be eligible for both the maximum AOTC credit (all else equal) and it will be eligible to exclude all of its grants from income. If, however, a family's tuition, required fees and books minus its scholarships is less than $4,000, the family needs to decide whether to use the "excess" grants to pay living expenses which would make them taxable or to pay AOTC eligible expenses which would reduce the family's AOTC but allow the grants to be excluded from gross income.

Generally, because the first $2,000 of eligible expenses paid by a family has a very high effective credit rate, most families will optimize their benefits by paying at least $2,000 of AOTC eligible expenses themselves even if it means using their scholarships to pay expenses that are not excludable from income.[31] Whether a family is also better off paying the next $2,000 of AOTC eligible expenses themselves, even if it means using their scholarships to pay living expenses, depends on whether or not the marginal tax rate of the student and family is higher than the effective credit rate for the second $2,000 of expenses. The effective credit rate on the second $2,000 of eligible expenses is much lower than the first $2,000 of eligible expenses.[32] For families where the student is a dependent, Pell Grants included in income would most likely be taxed at a marginal rate of 10% (and even then only to the extent the student's income exceeds the standard deduction for dependents). For families where the student is the primary or secondary filer, calculating the relative benefit of AOTC eligible expenses in excess of $2,000 may be more complicated if income is in the phase-out rate of the EITC (where their marginal tax rate is very high).

Example 1 illustrates the simplest case where the family has no EITC and sufficient tuition, required fees and book expenses to minimize the interaction between Pell Grants and the AOTC. In this example, the family has total wages of $42,000 – $40,000 attributable to the parent and $2,000 attributable to the student – and a Pell Grant of $1,800. The student has tuition, required

---

[31] The effective credit rate for the first $2,000 of AOTC expenses ranges from 40% for families without tax liability (before the AOTC) to 100% for families with tax liability.
[32] The effective credit rate for the second $2,000 of AOTC eligible expenses is as low as 10% for families that are only eligible for the refundable portion of the AOTC.

fees and books of $9,550. In such a case, if the family uses the entire Pell Grant to pay for tuition, required fees and books, there are still more than $4,000 of AOTC eligible expenses that are paid by the parent. Because scholarships used to pay tuition, required fees, and books are not taxable, the child's total income is still equal to the initial $2,000 of wage income, which is well below the filing threshold for dependent filers. With $40,000 of wages earned by the parent, the family qualifies for the full $2,500 AOTC ($1,000 of which is refundable). The parent's total income tax liability is $508. The family's total Federal tax and grant benefits (including the Pell and the AOTC)) are $4,300, leaving $13,250 (76 percent) of tuition, fees, books, living expenses unreimbursed.

Table 11
Examples of Interaction Between Pell Grant and AOTC in 2011
Head of Household with One Child Who Attends College Full Time

	Parent Earns $40,000 Child Earns $2,000			Parent Earns $20,000 Child Earns $2,000		
	Example 1	Example 2	Example 3	Example 4	Example 5	Example 6
Tuition, Required Fees and Books	9,550	4,000	2,000	9,550	4,000	2,000
Room and Board	8,000	8,000	8,000	8,000	8,000	8,000
Total Pell Grants	1,800	1,800	1,800	5,550	5,550	5,550
Pell Used to Pay Tuition, Required Fees and Books	1,800	0	0	5,550	0	0
Pell Used to Pay Living Expenses	0	1,800	1,800	0	5,550	5,550
Expenses Eligible for AOTC (up to $4,000)	4,000	4,000	2,000	4,000	4,000	2,000
Tax Calculation if Student Receives a Pell Grant						
Parent's Return						
Total Income	40,000	40,000	40,000	20,000	20,000	20,000
Taxable Income[1]	24,100	24,100	24,100	4,100	4,100	4,100
Tax Before Credits	3,008	3,008	3,008	410	410	410
AOTC	2,500	2,500	2,000	1,410	1,410	1,210
EITC	0	0	0	2,565	2,565	2,565
Tax Liability of Parent[2]	508	508	1,008	-3,565	-3,565	-3,365
Student's Return[3]						
Total Income	2,000	3,800	3,800	2,000	7,550	7,550
Taxable Income	0	0	0	0	1,750	1,750
Tax Liability of Student	0	0	0	0	175	175
Total Tax Liability if Student Receives a Pell Grant	508	508	1,008	-3,565	-3,390	-3,190
Tax Calculation if Student Does Not Receive a Pell Grant						
Parent's Return						
Tax Before Credits	3,008	3,008	3,008	410	410	410
AOTC	2,500	2,500	2,000	1,410	1,410	1,210
EITC	0	0	0	2,565	2,565	2,565
Tax Liability of Parent[2]	508	508	1,008	-3,565	-3,565	-3,365
Student's Return[3]						
Tax Liability of Student	0	0	0	0	0	0
Total Tax Liability if Student Does Not Receive a Pell Pell Grant	508	508	1,008	-3,565	-3,565	-3,365
Summary						
Increase in Tax Liability (or Decrease in Outlay) Because the Student Receives a Pell Grant	0	0	0	0	175	175
Total Tax and Grant Benefits[4]	4,300	4,300	3,800	9,525	9,350	9,150
Unreimbursed Tuition, Fees, Books, and Living Expenses	13,250	7,700	6,200	8,025	2,650	850
-- As a % of Total Tuition, Fees, Books and Living Expenses	75.5	64.2	62.0	45.7	22.1	8.5

footnotes on following page

Examples 2 and 3 show families that benefit most when the Pell Grant is used to pay for living expenses and included in the student's income for tax purposes. Because the family has sufficient tax liability, they receive a $1 tax credit for each $1 of AOTC eligible expense up to $2,000 and then they receive 25 cents for each additional $1 of AOTC eligible expenses (over $2,000) up to $4,000. For any level of tuition, required fees, and books less than $4,000, the family will maximize its tax and grant benefits by using the entire Pell Grant to pay living expenses. In Example 2, tuition, required fees and books are $4,000. If the Pell Grant pays for living expenses, the student's taxable income rises to $3,800 (the sum of wages plus included Pell Grant) but the student's tax liability remains zero. The family's total tax and grant benefits is $4,300. Of the family's total education expenses (tuition, fees, books, living expenses), $7,770 (64.2 percent) are not reimbursed. In Example 3, tuition, required fees and books are only $2,000 so the AOTC is only $2,000 and total tax and grant benefits are $3,800.

Examples 4 through 6 repeat Examples 1 through 3 except that the taxpayer has earnings of only $20,000 and therefore qualifies for a maximum Pell Grant of $5,550 and an EITC. In Example 4, where the family's tuition, required fees and books minus its Pell Grant exceeds $4,000, the family can still exclude the Pell Grant from income and have $4,000 of AOTC eligible expenses. Because the AOTC is partially refundable, the family is eligible for an AOTC of $1,410. Total tax and grant benefits (including the Pell, EITC, and AOTC) are $9,525; only $8,025 (46%) of total tuition, fees, books, living expenses are unreimbursed.

35

In Example 5, the family's tuition, required fees and books are equal to the maximum eligible expenses for the AOTC. For this family, any level of AOTC expenses between $2,250 and $4,000 results in the same tax liability. This example illustrates the specific case if the family pays all $4,000 of tuition out of pocket, includes the full Pell Grant in income and then uses it to pay living expenses. The parent's return looks as it did in Example 4. However, the student's income increases to $7,550 due to the inclusion of the Pell Grant. After allowing for the appropriate standard deduction, the student owes income taxes of $175 on $1,750 of taxable income and must file a dependent return. The family receives an AOTC of $1410. The family's total tax and grant benefits, net of the additional tax paid by the student, is $9,350.[33]

In Example 6, tuition expenses are only $2,000. The family maximizes benefits by using the entire Pell Grant to pay living expenses so that the full $2,000 is available for the AOTC. The effective credit rate on the first $2,000 of AOTC for families whose nonrefundable credit is constrained by income is 40%, significantly in excess of the 10% marginal tax rate faced by the student.

---

[33] The effective credit rate for a family whose nonrefundable AOTC dollars are constrained by income is 10%, (40% of the 25% credit rate) on expenses between $2,000 and $4,000. Because the student's tax liability also increases by 10 cents per dollar of expense, all allocations in this range result in the same benefit. If the family would prefer to keep the student below the filing threshold of $5,800, thus simplifying the return, only $3,800 of the Pell Grant should be allocated to income and the remaining $1,750 of the Pell Grant allocated to education expenses. This leaves $2,250 of education expenses to be paid out of pocket and thus eligible for an AOTC. The family will receive an AOTC of $1,235, which is identical to the AOTC net of the tax increase to the student as presented in the table. If education expenses allocated to the AOTC are below $2,250, the family can increase their allocation to the AOTC without increasing the student's tax liability.

Table 12
Examples of Interaction Between Pell Grant and AOTC in 2011
Head of Household Filer with One Child. Filer Attends College Full Time

	Parent-Student Earns $20,000		
	Example 7	Example 8	Example 9
Tuition, Required Fees and Books	9,550	4,000	2,000
Room and Board	8,000	8,000	8,000
Total Pell Grants	5,550	5,550	5,550
Pell Used to Pay Tuition, Required Fees and Books	5,550	2,000	0
Pell Used to Pay Living Expenses	0	3,550	5,550
Expenses Eligible for AOTC (up to $4,000)	4,000	2,000	2,000
Tax Calculation if Student Receives a Pell Grant			
Filer's Return			
Total Income	20,000	23,550	25,550
Taxable Income[1]	4,100	7,650	9,650
Tax Before Credits	410	765	965
AOTC	1,410	1,565	1,765
EITC	2,565	1,998	1,678
Child Credit	1,000	1,000	1,000
Total Tax Liability if Student Receives a Pell Grant[2]	-4,565	-3,798	-3,478
Tax Calculation if Student Does Not Receive a Pell Grant			
Filer's Return			
Tax Before Credits	410	410	410
AOTC	1,410	1,410	1,210
EITC	2,565	2,565	2,565
Child Credit	1,000	1,000	1,000
Tax Liability if Student Does Not Receive a Pell Grant[2]	-4,565	-4,565	-4,365
Summary			
Increase in Tax Liability (or Decrease in Outlay) Because the Student Receives a Pell Grant[3]	0	767	887
Total Tax and Grant Benefits for Education[4]	6,960	6,193	5,873
Unreimbursed Tuition, Fees, Books, and Living Expenses	10,590	5,807	4,127
-- As a % of Total Tuition, Fees, Books and Living Expenses	60.3	48.4	41.3

footnotes on following page

Examples 7, 8, and 9 in Table 12 present the interactions between the Pell Grant and the AOTC in the case of a family where the student is a head of household filer with one young dependent child. In this case, the Pell Grant is income to the taxpayer which in turn affects his or her tax liability. As in Examples 4, 5, and 6, the parent has an income of \$20,000, entirely from wages, receives the maximum Pell Grant of \$5,550, and an EITC. The EITC is not an education benefit in these three examples because the qualifying child's benefits do not rely on his or her education status (the student is the parent).[34] Because the family in these three examples is in the phase out range of the EITC, their marginal tax rate is 25.98%[35] and the level of EITC will be affected by the amount of the Pell Grant included in income. Each \$1 of grant aid added to income will increase the family's tax liability (decrease their outlay) by almost 26 cents. In contrast, they receive 40 cents for each \$1 of AOTC eligible expenses up to \$2,000 of expenses and 20 cents for each additional \$1 of AOTC eligible expenses (over \$2,000) up to a total of \$4,000 of expenses.[36]

---

[34] In the case of a dependent student, the age threshold for the EITC is increased from 19 to 23, thus the EITC is an education benefit in Table 11. Table 12, describes a nontraditional student, for whom the EITC is not an education benefit.

[35] The marginal tax rate in this example will not hold for all taxpayers or all taxpayers with an EITC. Marginal tax rates vary and depend on a taxpayer's source and level of income and family composition as well as other factors.

[36] The 20 cents per dollar consists of 40% ×25% refundable plus 10% nonrefundable.

In Example 7, where the family's tuition, required fees and books minus its Pell Grant exceeds $4,000, the family can still exclude the Pell Grant from income and have $4,000 of AOTC eligible expenses. Because the AOTC is only partially refundable, the family is only eligible for an AOTC of $1,410. Total tax and grant benefits (including the Pell and AOTC) are $6,960. $10,590 (60.3%) of total tuition, fees, books, living expenses are unreimbursed.

In Examples 8 and 9, the family's tuition, required fees and books minus its Pell Grant are less than $4,000. It is not possible for the student to exclude the student's entire Pell Grant and have $4,000 of AOTC eligible expenses. Moreover, because the family's marginal tax rate is almost 26%, the AOTC for the first $2,000 of AOTC eligible expenses is more valuable than excluding the Pell Grant from income but the AOTC for the second $2,000 of AOTC eligible expense is not as valuable as excluding the Pell Grant from income. Consequently in these examples, the taxpayer maximizes tax benefits by using the Pell Grant to pay tuition, required fees, and books in excess of $2,000 and the remainder to pay for living expenses.

To maximize benefits when tuition is $4,000 as in Example 8, the family should use $2,000 of the Pell Grant to pay tuition, required fees, and books and $3,550 to pay for living expenses. This allocation does not maximize expenses eligible for the AOTC, but it does maximize the combined benefit of the AOTC and the EITC after accounting for the interaction of these benefits with taxable income. The family's total tax and grant benefits net of the lower refund because a portion of the Pell was taxable is $6,193. Of the family's total education expenses (tuition, fees, books, living expenses) $5,807 (48 percent) are not reimbursed.

In Example 9, the family's wage income is unchanged but the student attends a school with tuition equal to $2,000. The family maximizes its tax benefits by using the entire Pell Grant to pay living expenses. The family's total tax and grant benefits net of the effects of the Pell Grant on taxable income is $5,873. Of the family's total education expenses (tuition, fees, books, living expenses) $4,127 (40.3 percent) are not reimbursed.

Box 1

Families that Misallocate their Expenses May Leave Money on the Table

Families can choose to use their Pell Grant to pay tuition, required fees and books, or they can use it to pay living expenses. In the examples shown in Table 11, the families allocate the Pell Grant to maximize their total tax and Pell Grant benefits. But what would happen if the family didn't get it right?

Let's look at the family in Example 5. This family has earned income of $22,000 ($20,000 earned by the taxpayer, and $2,000 by the dependent student). The family has $4,000 of expenses for tuition, required fees, and books and receives the maximum Pell Grant of $5,550. If the family paid their entire tuition with the Pell Grant, the family would not be eligible for any AOTC. If the family put the entire Pell Grant toward living expenses, total benefits would be maximized, even though the total amount of tax is higher. Families that misallocate their expenses may leave money on the table.

Example 5: This family gets it right. The family uses the Pell Grant to pay the first $5,550 of living expenses. This leaves $4,000 of tuition expenses available for an AOTC of $1,410. The student's tax liability is $175.

Example 5a: This time the family uses the Pell Grant to pay all $4,000 of tuition, leaving no expenses eligible for the AOTC, and thus, receiving no credit. After accounting for differences in the tax liability of the student and the AOTC, by failing to optimize the family forfeits $1,235 in benefits.

	Example 5 The Right Approach	Example 5a Tuition, Fees, and Books
Total Pell Grants	5,550	5,550
Pell Used to Pay Tuition, Required Fees and Books	0	4,000
Pell Used to Pay Living Expenses	5,550	1,550
Expenses Eligible for AOTC (up to $4,000)	4,000	0
Total Income Parent	20,000	20,000
Taxable Income	4,100	4,100
Tax Before Credits	410	410
AOTC	1,410	0
EITC	2,565	2,565
Tax Liability of Parent[1]	-3,565	-2,155
Total Income Student	7,550	3,550
Taxable Income	1,750	0
Tax Liability of Student	175	0
Total Tax Liability of Family	-3,390	-2,155
Total Tax and Grant Benefits[2]	9,350	8,115
Net Loss from Failing to Optimize Benefits		1,235

[1] Negative values indicate that the family is receiving a refund.

[2] Total tax and grant benefits equals the sum of the AOTC and EITC calculated as if the student did not receive a Pell Grant minus the increase in tax liability (decrease in outlay) because the student used some or all of the grant to pay living expenses.

Box 2

Allocating Expenses is Even More Complicated for Non-Traditional Students

Families can choose to use their Pell Grant to pay tuition, required fees and books, or they can use it to pay living expenses. In the examples shown in Table 12, the families allocate the Pell Grant to maximize their total tax and Pell Grant benefits. But what would happen if the family didn't get it right?

Let's look at the family in Example 8. This family has earned income of $20,000 and $4,000 of expenses for tuition, required fees, and books. They receive the maximum Pell Grant of $5,550. If the family paid their entire tuition with the Pell Grant, the family would not be eligible for any AOTC. If the family put the entire Pell Grant toward living expenses, AOTC would be maximized, but at the expense of other benefits. Families that misallocate their expenses may leave money on the table.

Example 8: This family gets it right. Although they have enough expenses to claim a larger AOTC, the family claims just enough education expenses to maximize total benefits after accounting for tax liability, the AOTC and the EITC.

Example 8a: This time the family uses the Pell Grant to pay all $4,000 of tuition, leaving no expenses eligible for the AOTC, and thus, receiving no credit. After accounting for differences in tax liability, the AOTC and the EITC, by failing to optimize they forfeit $1,045 in benefits.

Example 8b: This time the family uses the Pell Grant to pay the first $5,550 of living expenses. AOTC is maximized, but after accounting for differences in tax liability, the AOTC and the EITC, by failing to optimize they forfeit $120 in benefits.

	Example 8 The Right Mix	Example 8a Tuition Fees Books	Example 8b Room and Board
Total Pell Grants	5,550	5,550	5,550
Pell Used to Pay Tuition, Required Fees and Books	2,000	4,000	0
Pell Used to Pay Living Expenses	3,550	1,550	5,550
Expenses Eligible for AOTC (up to $4,000)	2,000	0	4,000
Total Income	23,550	21,550	25,550
Taxable Income	7,650	5,650	9,650
Tax Before Credits	765	565	965
AOTC	1,565	0	1,965
EITC	1,998	2,317	1,678
Child Credit	1,000	1,000	1,000
Tax Liability[1]	-3,798	-2,752	-3,678
Total Tax and Grant Benefits for Education[2]	6,193	5,147	6,073
Net Loss from Failing to Optimize Benefits		-1,045	-120

[1] Negative values indicate that the family is receiving a refund

[2] "Total Tax and Grant Benefits for Education" equals the sum of the AOTC calculated as if the student did not receive a Pell Grant plus the Pell Grant minus the increase in tax liability (decrease in outlay) if the student used some or all of their Pell Grant to pay living expenses. The increase in tax liability includes the effect of including the Pell Grant in income on EITC.

41

B. Graphical Representation of Interaction

Figures 2 and 3 show the value of Pell Grants and the main education tax benefits for hypothetical families at two representative levels of tuition and qualified expenses ($2,500 and $7,500) as income is increased. In these examples, the families consist of two married adults and their dependent college-aged child. The child attends school full-time. These two levels of tuition and qualified expenses were chosen because they are close to the average levels in 2010, where $2,500 was the average tuition at public community college and $7,500 was the average tuition level at a public four-year college.[37] Although these amounts do not explicitly consider the value of books and fees (which are also qualifying expenses for the AOTC), the amounts are broadly representative of the qualified expenses faced by students at these types of institutions, many of whom will have received additional aid from the institutions or from state governments. The $2,500 case is important because it captures the experience of families who face limitations on aid eligibility due to limited tuition expenses. Families are assumed to have only wage income, and are assumed to have a typical level of deductible expenses.[38] For purposes of computing the Pell Grant, it is assumed that the student is beginning his or her education this year, and thus received neither a Pell Grant nor an education credit the previous year. It is also assumed that the families have few additional assets. Pell Grant amounts and income tax liabilities would vary if these simple assumptions were changed. In these figures, families allocate their Pell Grant between living expenses and tuition in the way that maximizes total benefits. It is also assumed that the student earns no income and remains below the filing threshold for dependent filers.[39]

Taking Figure 2 as an example, total Federal benefits by provision are shown for a hypothetical family with $2,500 in tuition (fees, and qualifying expenses) as income increases. Pell Grants, the AOTC, the EITC and the dependency exemption are shown.

---

[37] See notes to Table 1.

[38] The Office of Tax Analysis routinely assumes that itemized deductions are equal to 18 percent of most forms of income. Each family is assumed to itemize deductions only if doing so reduces its Federal income taxes (i.e., if the itemized deductions exceed the standard deduction).

[39] This assumption simplifies the exposition considerably, but has little qualitative effect on the figures. The effect of adding student earnings will be considered at the end of the discussion of Figure 2.

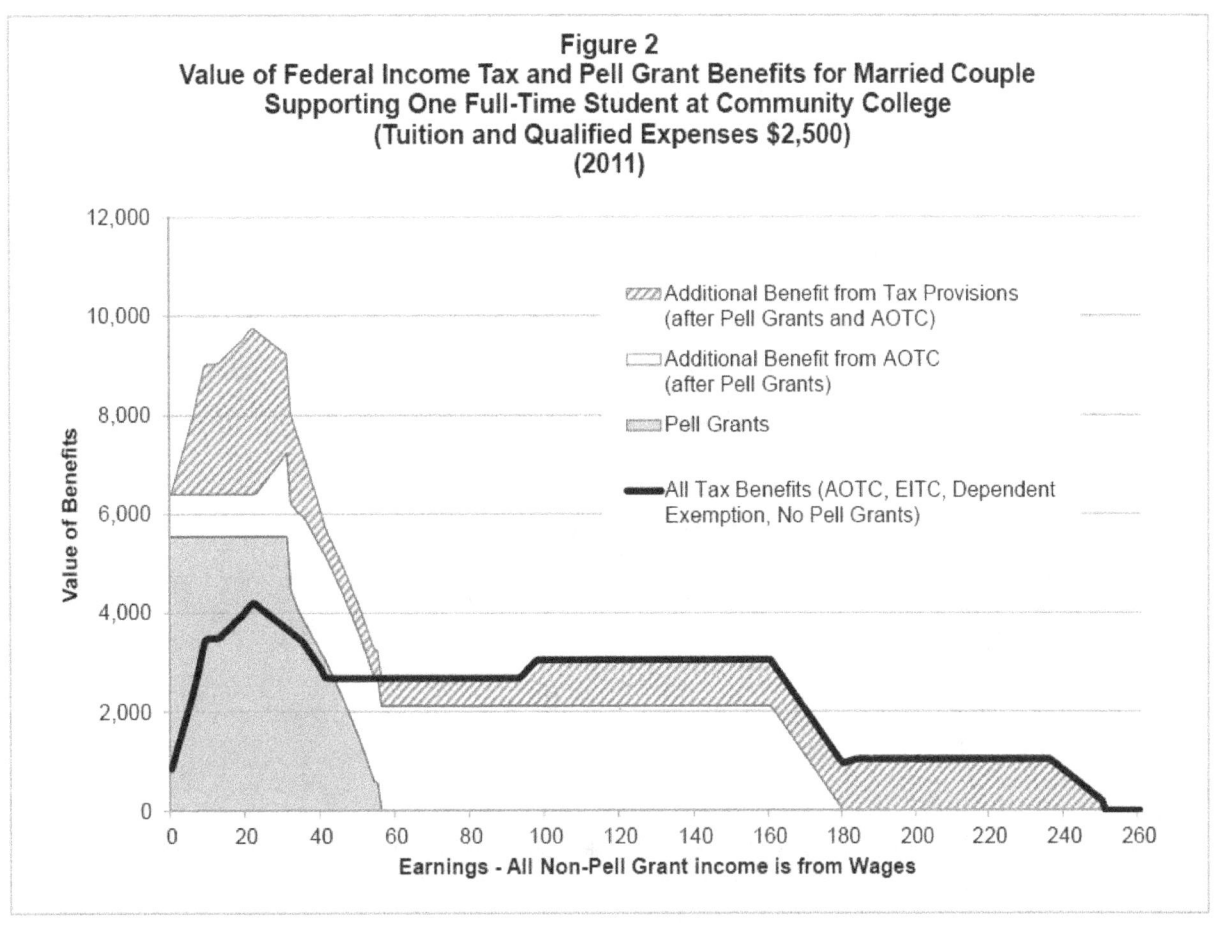

Figure 2
Value of Federal Income Tax and Pell Grant Benefits for Married Couple
Supporting One Full-Time Student at Community College
(Tuition and Qualified Expenses $2,500)
(2011)

The solid black line (bottom) shows the value of all tax benefits as income increases, ignoring any interactions with the Pell Grant. This is equivalent to the case where the family does not receive a Pell Grant. The family would be eligible for three main tax benefits, which when summed, are equal to the black line. First, the family would be eligible for the non-refundable dependency exemption deduction, which increases in value with the taxpayer's marginal tax rate; taxpayers on the alternative minimum tax (AMT) lose the benefit of the personal exemptions, as can be seen by the decrease at the highest incomes shown. Second, the family would be eligible for the earned income credit, which phases in with the first dollar of wage income, plateaus, and then phases out at nearly $36,100 of income. Third, the family would be eligible for a partially refundable AOTC. At this level of tuition, the family would be eligible for a maximum AOTC of $2,125. At low incomes, the family would be constrained by income tax liability. Only $850 of the AOTC would be refundable, which means that taxpayers earning less than $35,450 would receive less than the full amount of the credit. (Married filers with one dependent child would not have $1,275 of tax liability before credits until earning $35,450.) At higher incomes, between $160,000 and $180,000, the AOTC phases out.

The three areas show the cumulative value of the Pell Grant and successive tax benefits as more tax benefits are added. The gray block shows the value of the Pell Grant. Because, in 2011, families of dependent students with income of $32,000 or less automatically qualify for a maximum Pell Grant, there is a cliff at $32,000 of income where the calculated value of the Pell Grant using the formulas is much less than the automatic maximum grant.

The gray area plus the white area combines the value of the Pell Grant and the AOTC. The spike at incomes between $20,000 and $30,000 occurs because the nonrefundable portion of the AOTC is phasing in with tax liability. (The value of the AOTC continues to rise until $35,450 but the Pell Grant declines.) The white area does not include the value of the dependency exemption deduction or the EITC.[40]

Finally, adding the gray area, the white area and the striped area together combines the value of all benefits, including the EITC and the dependency exemption deduction. For families with AGI below $39,000, the additional tax benefits shown by the striped area are mostly due to the EITC. For families with AGI above $41,000, the additional tax benefits are exclusively due to the value of the dependency exemption deduction which increases with the statutory rate and then phases out as the family begins to pay the AMT. If the student had additional earnings besides the Pell Grant, the student is likely to have a small amount of tax liability. For example, a student who earns $2,000 at a part-time job and receives the maximum Pell Grant would have $1,750 of income above the $5,800 standard deduction for dependent filers.[41] This income would result in additional tax liability for the family of $175. As family incomes increase, Pell Grants decrease (and thus the effect of the Pell Grant on the student's total earnings), until the student's earnings drop below the filing threshold at incomes above $35,000. The total value of

---

[40] Few taxpayers would actually receive the values shown by the white area. It is included to highlight the distinction between the AOTC and the two age-based tax benefits. (Eligibility for the EITC and the exemption for a dependent child are restricted to full-time students under 24 years of age.)
[41] The standard deduction is substantially lower for dependent filers with unearned income.

benefits would drop at the effected incomes, with an effect on total benefits always below 3 percent.

Figure 3 repeats Figure 2 for the case where tuition and expenses equal $7,500. Most differences between the two figures are relatively small; larger tuition expenses results in a slightly larger AOTC (for households not constrained by income tax liability), and a resulting decrease in the amount of the Pell Grant that would be included in the income of the student.

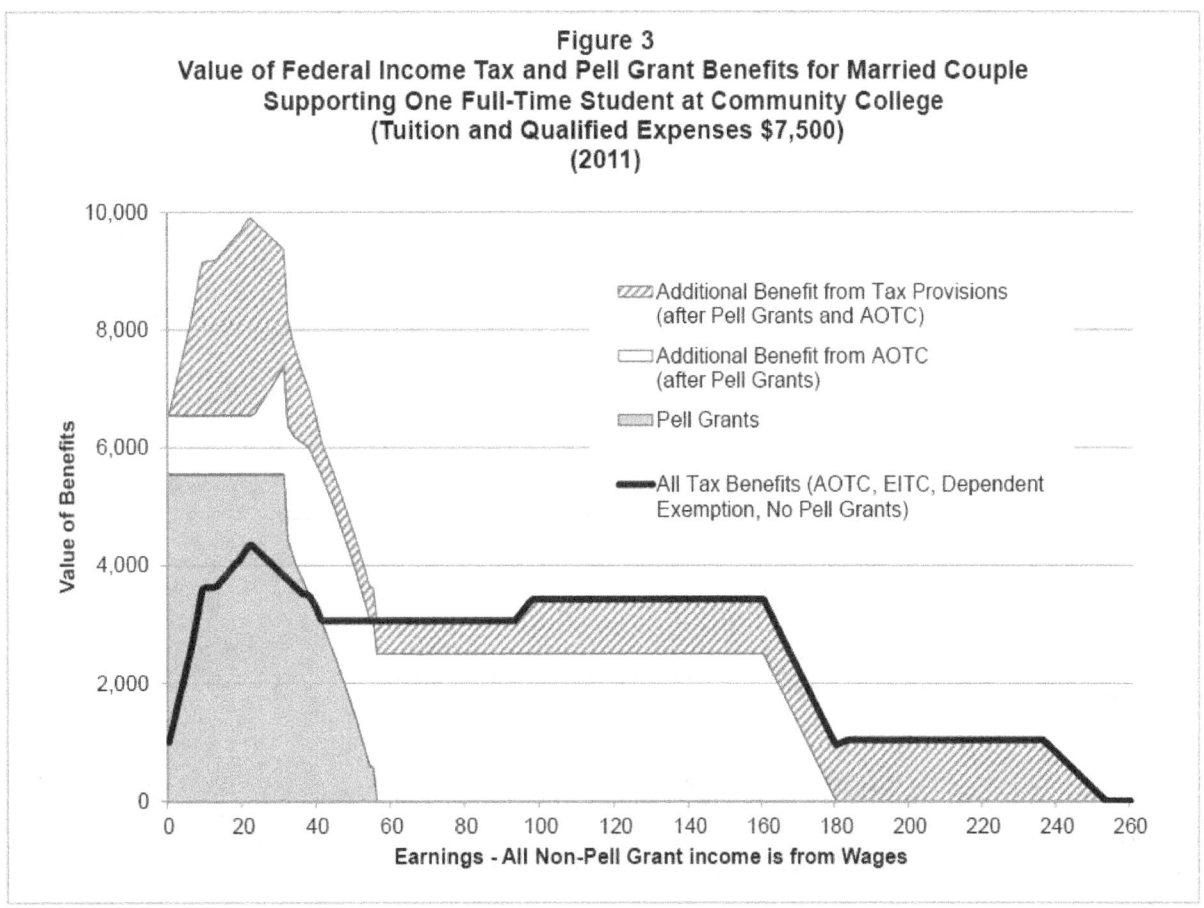

Figure 3
Value of Federal Income Tax and Pell Grant Benefits for Married Couple
Supporting One Full-Time Student at Community College
(Tuition and Qualified Expenses $7,500)
(2011)

Figure 4 presents the case of a family consisting of two married adults, one of whom attends community college full-time, and their young dependent child. As in Figure 2, the student has tuition and qualified expenses of $2,500. However, in this case the student is the taxpayer and not a dependent. This difference has a big effect on the amount of student-related benefits received by the family. First, the AOTC is the only tax benefit the family receives. The EITC and the dependency exemption are not considered tax benefits for education in this case because the family would still be eligible for these benefits if the parent were not in school. Second, the Pell Grant is included as income of the taxpayer (to the extent that it is not spent on tuition or other excludable expenses) and not as the dependent's income. As a result the Pell Grant can affect the amount of EITC and AOTC the family is entitled to receive, and the Pell Grant is more likely to be taxed. As discussed in the text accompanying Table 12 and Box 2, maximizing expenses eligible for the AOTC, may not maximize the combined benefit of the AOTC and the EITC after accounting for the interaction of these benefits with taxable income.

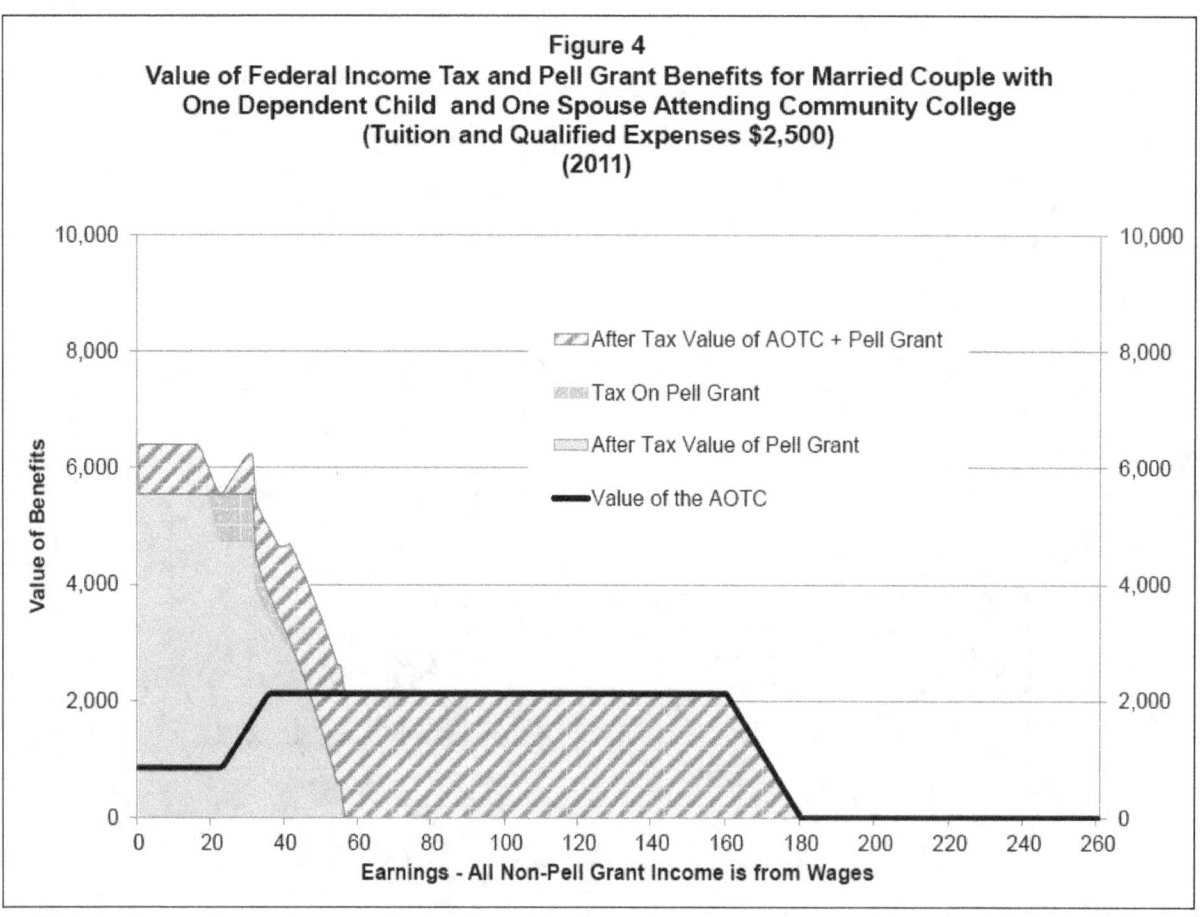

Figure 4
Value of Federal Income Tax and Pell Grant Benefits for Married Couple with One Dependent Child and One Spouse Attending Community College (Tuition and Qualified Expenses $2,500)
(2011)

The solid black line shows the value of the AOTC as income increases, ignoring any interactions with the Pell Grant. This is equivalent to the case where the family does not receive a Pell Grant. The family is eligible strictly for the refundable portion of the AOTC until income exceeds the filing threshold of $22,700. The AOTC phases out beginning at incomes of $160,000.

The grey areas (dark and light) sum to the statutory value of the Pell Grant, with the darker area representing the tax due to the inclusion in income of any Pell Grant in excess of tuition, fees and qualified expenses. The light gray area is the value of the Pell Grant net of the tax. This is equivalent to the case where the family does not receive an AOTC.

The sum of the striped region and the gray region is the total amount of benefit this family will receive after accounting for all resulting changes in tax liability, including the effect of the Pell Grant on the phase-out of the EITC. The spike at incomes between $20,000 and $30,000 occurs because the nonrefundable portion of the AOTC is phasing in with tax liability. Recall that including a portion of the Pell Grant in income has an effect on a number of provisions. If the family is in the phase-out range of the EITC, the additional income would lower the value of the EITC (for this family, at a rate of 15.98 percent). The family's tax liability (if positive) would increase (most likely at a marginal rate of 10 percent for families receiving a Pell Grant). However the family's AOTC might also increase if the otherwise allowable credit had been constrained by their income tax liability. The extent to which the total area (striped plus light and dark gray) is less than the sum of the gray areas and the area under the black line (sum not pictured) is due to these interactions.

VI. Other Coordination Issues

A. Smaller than Expected AOTC Benefits

As the foregoing discussion illustrates, there are myriad tax benefits and spending programs to subsidize higher education. Confusion about the different programs may prevent students from receiving the full benefit to which they are entitled. Currently, there are three main tax-based benefits for current year expenses: the AOTC, the Lifetime Learning Credit, and the tuition and fees deduction. While many taxpayers are eligible for more than one benefit, taxpayers are restricted to one benefit per student each year. Recent work examining the selection between two tax-based benefits finds that a substantial number of taxpayers do not select the benefit that offers the largest reduction in tax liability.[42] Replacing the existing set of tax-based benefits with a single coherent benefit could increase the number of students and families who realize their maximum allowable tax benefit. Recent work finds evidence that complex student aid applications are a deterrent to program use, and the same is likely true of tax benefits for education.[43]

Interactions between tax benefits and grant programs are complicated, and may also prevent taxpayers from receiving the full benefit to which they are entitled. For students who receive both a Pell Grant and an AOTC, the portion of expenses for tuition, required fees and books paid with money from the Pell Grant does not count for the purposes of calculating the AOTC. Given current information reporting (primarily Form 1098-T) one does not know the extent to which taxpayers are optimizing as assumed in the examples in the preceding section, but it is likely that many do not.

Another reason that students may fail to realize the full value of their AOTC is that tax-based federal student benefits may be offset by increases in the price of attending college. To the extent that colleges and universities respond to the AOTC by increasing their prices, the AOTC becomes a transfer to institutions of higher learning rather than lowering the cost of postsecondary attendance for students and their families. There is little evidence that colleges and universities *increase tuition* in response to student grant aid programs.[44] However, recent work finds that some 4-year colleges and universities increase the net price they receive by *decreasing school grant aid*.[45] Lowering grant aid for AOTC recipients may be one method that college administrators use to cope with constrained endowments and reduced state support for higher education.[46] Even if colleges and universities offset the intended cost reduction of

---

[42] See Turner (2010A).

[43] See Bettinger, et al. (2009).

[44] See Long (2006) and GAO (2002).

[45] See Turner (2010B).

[46] Analyzing 842 university endowments, the National Association of College and University Business Officers finds that in FY2008-FY2009 university endowments dropped by an average of 19 percent. The average three year growth ending in FY2009 was -2.5 percent. Excerpts from the study can be found at: http://www.nacubo.org/Documents/research/2009_NCSE_Press_Release.pdf. The Center for the Study of Education Policy reports that in FY2008-FY2009, state support for higher education dropped by an average of 3 percent. Statistics on state level support are available here: http://grapevine.illinoisstate.edu/index.shtml.

AOTC, students may still benefit from the programs if schools devote the captured aid towards expenditures that students value. For example, schools may increase expenditures on student services, capital improvements or make improvements to education quality.

B. Tax Compliance

Complicated tax and spending provisions and the lack of adequate third-party reporting may also lead to non-compliance. Currently, it is possible for non-compliant taxpayers to inappropriately reduce their income taxes by claiming an AOTC award that exceeds their maximum allowable credit. This is possible in part, because there is no third party verification for educational expenses that qualify for the AOTC. Schools are required to file Form 1098-T with the IRS, but this form does not include the amount of qualified educational expenses. As discussed above (Section IV), in Boxes 1 and 2 of the form, schools are required to report either "payments received" or "amounts billed" to both the IRS and to the eligible student. However, neither of these measures accurately characterizes the amount of education spending that qualifies for the AOTC. Qualified expenses that count towards the AOTC include tuition and fees but these must be reduced by tax-free student grant aid and any distributions from tax-free education spending accounts. Other expenses that qualify for the AOTC, such as spending on books, supplies and equipment, are not subject to third party verification. Research on tax compliance finds evidence of greater tax avoidance in the absence of third party verification.[47] Adopting a different definition of qualified expenses that includes only third party verified spending, and requiring colleges and universities to report this spending directly to the IRS and to the student is likely to increase tax compliance by increasing the visibility of these amounts.

---

[47] See, for example, Kleven et. al. (2010), Mazur and Plumley (2007), and U.S. Internal Revenue Service (1996 and 2012).

VII. Options for Increased Coordination

As reflected in the overview above, the various education tax incentives and outlay programs under current law are numerous, overlapping, and complex. The programs vary in terms of who may receive benefits, which expenses may be covered, and how large an exclusion, deduction, or credit may be allowed. In recent years, however, there have been a number of advances that have made the process of applying for and receiving direct aid and tax credits easier.

Prior to the creation of the AOTC, students had to evaluate the Hope Scholarship, LLC, and tuition deduction to see which offered the greatest benefit. With the introduction of the AOTC, the choice is much simpler. The AOTC always confers the highest benefit, so students that are eligible for the AOTC are always better off choosing the AOTC over the LLC or tuition deduction.[48] The LLC and tuition deduction remain in the tax code for those students who do not qualify for the AOTC, including students attending school less than half-time and students who have completed their first four years of postsecondary education or who have claimed the AOTC for more than four taxable years.

The Administration has also succeeded in enhancing a web-based Free Application for Federal Student Aid (FAFSA). Ninety-nine percent of FAFSAs in 2010-2011 were submitted using the online application which no longer requires low-income students to provide asset information (information that was not used to determine their eligibility). The web form uses skip logic, text pop-ups and an IRS Data Match tool that, for eligible students, automatically populates, transfers, and verifies applicant tax data with the IRS in real-time, further streamlining the process for students and their families.

In addition, since May 2009, the Department of Education has provided instant estimates of Pell Grant and student loan eligibility. These estimates allow students to know in advance what

---

[48] In 2009, the first year of enactment, some students eligible for Midwestern disaster relief (which doubled the size of the maximum allowable Hope or lifetime learning credit) would have been better off choosing a Hope credit or LLC instead of the AOTC. This provision has since expired, so that in 2010 and thereafter, the AOTC confers the highest benefit for all students eligible for multiple benefits.

education benefits they can expect, increasing the likelihood that these benefits will affect enrollment.

Still, further coordination and simplification of the financial aid system, both direct aid and tax incentives are possible. Some options, described in detail below include: 1) reforming the needs analysis formula and the FAFSA; 2) adding an estimate of AOTC eligibility when students apply for Pell Grants; 3) improving information reporting on grants to insure eligible students receive maximum AOTC benefits; 4) excluding Pell Grants from gross income for tax purposes; and 5) integrating the delivery of the refundable portion of the AOTC and the Title IV delivery system.

1. **Simplify the Financial Aid Formula and Remove the Asset Test.**

Under this option, only information available on tax forms would be used to fill out the FAFSA. The asset tests would be eliminated. The current web-based FAFSA has an IRS data retrieval tool that allows eligible applicants to access tax data to auto-populate many of the fields in the FAFSA application. [49] This greatly simplifies the application process since the data are retrieved and, with permission of the student, transferred into the appropriate place on the student's web application. The student does not have to search for his or her records and does not need to worry about whether or not he or she is reporting the appropriate amount. Moreover, this provides the Department of Education with "point-of-entry" verification that the correct information is being reported. This capability increases compliance while at the same time decreasing the cost of compliance, a benefit for both taxpayers and students, as well as institutions which have to verify information for a share of aid applicants.

The determination of need under current law, however, requires both tax information and asset data for all but the lowest income students. For FAFSA purposes, an asset is valued at the time of application and thus is not available on an individual income tax form and can therefore not be retrieved, or verified by the web-based application. Yet, studies have shown that eliminating the asset information and income adjustments would have little impact on the overall number or size

---

[49] Not all students are able to use the data retrieval tool, (e.g. dependent students whose parents are not required to file a tax return).

of Pell awards.[50] Among all 2009-2010 Pell recipients, only 2.4 percent of parents of dependent students and only 2.5 percent of independent students had assets values large enough to influence the size of their aid award.

Removing all the asset information and income adjustments would allow students to apply for aid using only the information found on their income tax forms. In combination with the IRS data retrieval tool, this could make the process of applying much simpler. The application process will have moved from a labor intensive process of answering over 120 questions by hand to being able to retrieve and auto-populate the application with relative ease.

2. Web Estimates of AOTC Eligibility

Under this option, students and their families would receive an estimate of their eligibility for an AOTC at the same time as they receive an estimate of their eligibility for Pell Grants and federal loans. When a student applies for financial aid using the web-based FAFSA, he or she currently receives a real-time estimate of his or her Pell Grant eligibility. This proposal would use the FAFSA information (prior year IRS data) to estimate his or her eligibility for an AOTC in the succeeding year. The estimate would rely on his or her income in the prior year (or family income if applicable) and might be different if such income changed significantly in the following year. Applicants would need to be warned of this possibility. There would also need to be a warning about the possible interaction of the AOTC with other grant aid (such as institutional grants).

Still, by showing the possibility of receiving an AOTC alongside the value of a Pell Grant, students would have a better sense of the total level of federal aid that they could expect to receive. Unless families are aware of the availability of the AOTC, it cannot encourage enrollment.

---

[50] See Dynarski and Scott-Clayton (2007) and Council of Economic Advisers (2009).

3. Improve Information Reporting

As currently designed, the 1098-T is a valuable source of information for both the IRS and the student. But, the design could be improved to make the computation of the credit easier for the student and to increase compliance with the rules.

For the IRS, the current report is invaluable as it identifies the pool of individuals that are eligible for the education credits. Only students enrolled at an eligible institution are eligible for either the LLC or the AOTC, and only those enrolled at least half time and who have not completed their first four years of postsecondary education are eligible for the AOTC. Without the information report, the IRS would not have a third-party verification of eligible students.

For students, the receipt of a 1098-T serves to notify them that they may be eligible for tax benefits. The 2011 *Instructions for the Student* that accompanies the student's copy of the 1098-T notifies students that *"You, or the person who can claim you as a dependent, may be able to claim and education credit on Form 1040 or 1040A for the qualified tuition and related expenses that were actually paid in 2011."*

Unfortunately, the 1098-T falls short in providing the correct information a student needs to calculate his or her eligible expenses for the LLC or AOTC.

First, schools only report tuition and fees required for enrollment (either amounts billed or payments received), not expenses for required course materials such as books. Under prior law, only tuition and fees required for enrollment were eligible for the Hope credit. Under current law, eligible expenses for the LLC are still restricted to tuition and fees required for enrollment but eligible expenses for the AOTC also include the costs of required course materials such as books. There is no third party verification on the 1098-T for required course materials for the purpose of calculating the education tax credit. These materials may be purchased from vendors not affiliated with the school. Yet, for the purpose of administering direct Federal student aid, schools are required to construct a budget for each student that includes an estimate of course materials. These estimates could be included separately on the 1098-T.

Second, taxpayers may only claim expenses that are actually paid by the taxpayer (or taxpayer's claimed dependent) during the tax year. However, because schools are allowed to report amounts billed (Box 2) instead of payments received (Box 1), the 1098-T filed for one tax year may include expenses that are paid in the following tax year or expenses that are never paid. For example, if an otherwise eligible student started taking college classes in January 2011 and he or she was billed in December 2010, the student's school could choose to report the amount as billed in 2010 on a 2010 Form 1098-T but if the student did not pay the bill until January 2011, then the expenses would not be eligible for a 2010 AOTC. Only if the December 2010 bill is paid in 2010 would the student be eligible for an AOTC in 2010.[51] Alternatively, if a student is billed for a class and it is reported as billed on a 1098-T but the student drops the class, he or she may receive a 1098-T for a class that was never attended or paid for. Although the student's 1098-T for the following year would show an adjustment to the prior year amount (Box 4), it would be too late to help the student file his or her current year taxes.

Third, even if the 1098-T reported payments received for qualified tuition and required fees for all students and if it separately reported related course materials (eligible for the AOTC but not the LLC), it would still fall short of easing the computation burden for the student because it does not also report payments received for other expenses, such as room and board, that qualify for direct student assistance but not tax benefits. As shown above in the examples in Table 11, Pell Grants (and other grant aid) may be used to pay room and board, as well as tuition and other expenses that qualify for the AOTC. Applying Pell Grants toward room and board may increase the amount of expenses eligible for an AOTC and may be advantageous to the student. However, the student would need to include the Pell Grant in income. Such a calculation is complicated without an information report to guide the taxpayer. If, however, the 1098-T provided payments received for qualified tuition and related expenses, a separate line for course materials (including books), and a third line for payments received for room and board and other expenses eligible for Federal student assistance, then an IRS worksheet could direct a student to the tax minimizing calculations and compliant expense amounts to include in income and the

---

[51] In the example the student's classes begin in January 2011. A student may claim an AOTC for 2010 for expenses paid in 2010 for academic classes that begin in 2010 or the first 3 months of 2011.

expenses to treat as eligible expenses for the AOTC. Although some students are not charged room and board by the school because they live off campus or at home, all students receiving Federal aid are assigned an estimate of living expenses that are used to determine eligibility for Federal aid. In the absence of room and board charges by the school, these estimates could be reported.

Under this option, schools would be required to report 1) payments for tuition, required fees, 2) an allowance for course materials, and 3) payments or an allowance for room and board and other expenses eligible for direct student aid. Schools would continue to provide information on grant assistance administered through the school. With this information, an IRS worksheet could guide the student to appropriately calculate their tax benefits.

While this option would increase compliance costs on the part of institutions, the dramatic increase in aid being directed at these institutions warrants increased oversight. The AOTC is expected to cost $22 billion in FY2012 and the Pell Grant Program is over $35 billion in FY2012. With nearly $60 billion dollars being used to support postsecondary education through these two programs alone, institutions should be full partners in ensuring that eligible students are able to maximize their benefits and comply with the tax law. Increasing compliance ensures that tax benefits are available for those for whom they were intended.

4. Exclude Pell Grants from Taxable Income

Under section 117 of the Internal Revenue Code as amended by the Tax Reform Act of 1986 (TRA86), a scholarship or fellowship grant received by a degree candidate is excludable from gross income to the extent that it is used for 1) tuition and fees required for enrollment or attendance of the student at a qualified educational institution and 2) fees, books, supplies and equipment required for courses of instruction at the qualified educational institution.

Under this option, Pell Grants would again be excludable from gross income even if the grant exceeded tuition, required fees, and course-related expenses. As discussed above, Pell Grants are targeted at very low-income families. Including Pell Grants that are used to pay living expenses as income may be a hardship for low-income families that receive Pell Grants and who owe tax on these amounts. In support of this option, we note that other low-income benefits used for living expenses such as the supplemental nutrition assistance program (SNAP) and temporary assistance for needy families (TANF) are not taxable.

Other scholarships would remain taxable to the extent that they were used to pay expenses other than tuition and required fees. This option would increase the coordination of the Pell Grant and other tax benefits since the receipt of a Pell Grant would never reduce a student's AOTC or EITC. It would also simplify the education tax benefit calculation for Pell recipients and their families since they would not have to calculate how much of their grant (if any) should be included in income.

Figure 5 below shows the benefit of excluding Pell Grants from income for a married couple with a dependent child and one spouse attending community college ($2,500 in tuition and fees) full-time. The black line shows current law, which includes the effect that including Pell in income has on other tax benefits. The dashed gray line shows the extra benefit that would be received by moderate-income families if Pell Grants were excluded from income.

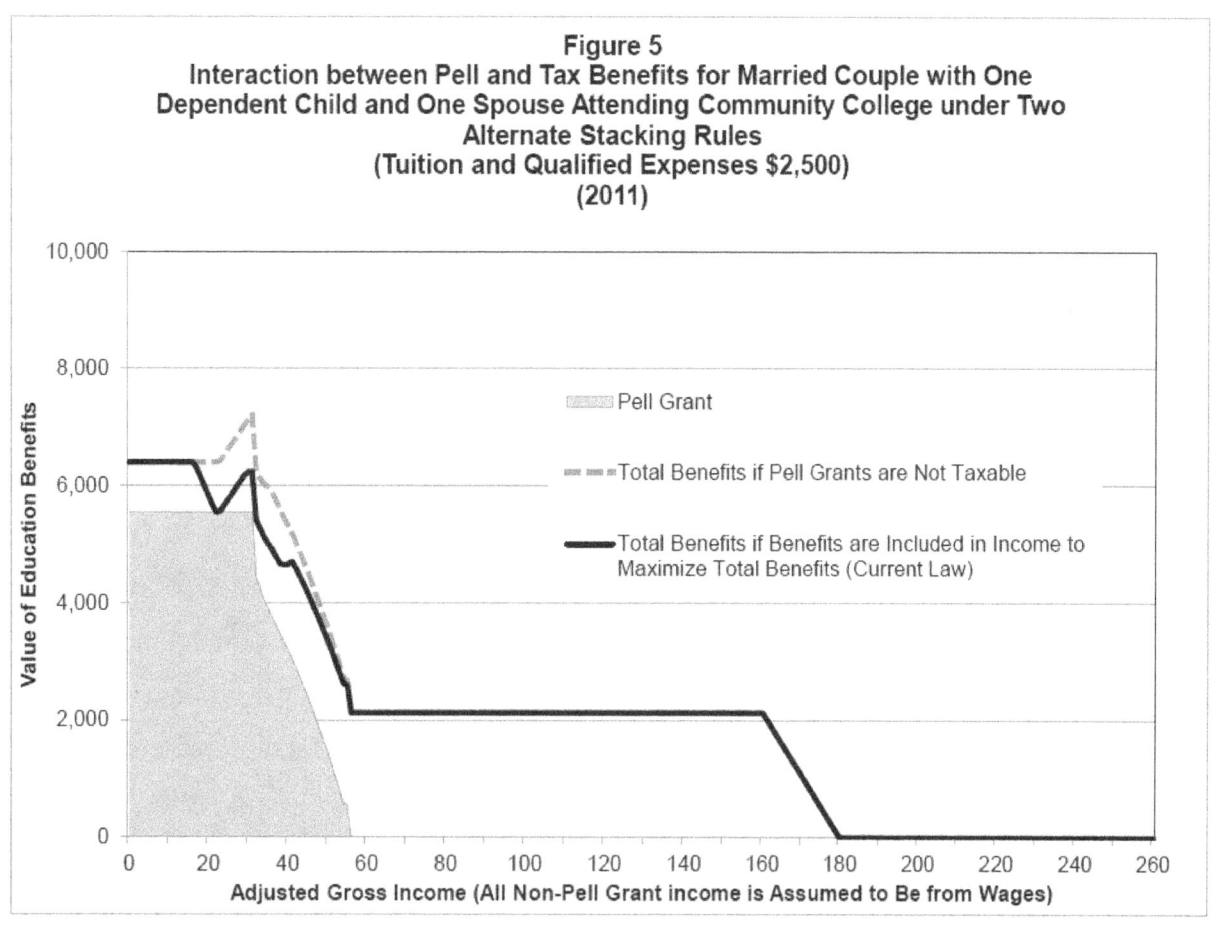

Figure 5
Interaction between Pell and Tax Benefits for Married Couple with One Dependent Child and One Spouse Attending Community College under Two Alternate Stacking Rules
(Tuition and Qualified Expenses $2,500)
(2011)

As shown in the figure, some low- and moderate-income families would benefit if Pell Grants were not taxable. In this example, families with income between $19,000 and $56,000 would have higher total benefits under the option. These amounts would vary by filing status, tuition level and other circumstances. Families with the lowest incomes would receive no additional tax benefit. In Figure 5, the greatest savings under this option is $955 for families with $34,000 of AGI (wages excluding Pell Grants).

Families supporting dependent students would see a reduction in tax to the extent that their dependent children had positive tax liability after considering the Pell Grant. However, all families would benefit from the simplification. This option would not affect the tax treatment of other scholarships. Excluding Pell Grants from income would be expected to cost less than $10 billion over ten years.

5. Integrate Delivery of the Refundable Portion of the AOTC into the Title IV Delivery System

Under this option, the refundable portion of the AOTC would be delivered to the student as a boost to their Pell grant rather than as a refundable tax credit. The AOTC-Pell boost would be based on prior year tax data as provided on the FAFSA and as verified by the IRS. The determination of the size of the AOTC-Pell boost and its delivery would be administered by the Department of Education. The nonrefundable portion of the AOTC would not be changed. Like the nonrefundable AOTC, the AOTC-Pell boost would only be available for four years.

There are significant advantages to administering the refundable portion of the AOTC through the Title IV Delivery System. One, the AOTC-Pell boost would be available to low-income students in a timely manner, and available at a time to influence a student's decision to enroll. Two, it could significantly reduce the compliance burden for the student and his or her family. As discussed in Section VIII below, administering an advanced refundable tax credit through the IRS would duplicate the efforts of the Department of Education by requiring students to submit to a second set of tests for eligibility in order to receive the tax benefit in advance. In contrast, under this option, the student would apply for both the Pell Grant and the AOTC-Pell boost using only the FAFSA.

One disadvantage to this program is that some students, for example those whose parent(s) experienced a reduction in income, might be eligible for an AOTC-Pell boost based on current year data but not based on prior year data. The Department of Education has mechanisms in place to address such changed circumstance and other grants and loans may be available in such cases.

VIII. Expedite Delivery of the AOTC -- Advance Refundability

As shown in Figures 2 through 5, the AOTC serves a wide range of families. Eligible low- and moderate- income families primarily receive a refundable credit of up to $1,000 (or 40 percent of the otherwise eligible amount). For families earning more (until the credit phases out at incomes in excess of $90,000 and $180,000 for single and joint filers respectively), the credit primarily offsets existing income tax liability.[52] Under current law, taxpayers who qualify for the AOTC and claim the credit receive the payment as part of their regular tax return filing. Thus, most taxpayers with eligible tuition expenses in 2010 would receive their credit in early- to mid-2011. For tuition paid in January, this could mean that taxpayers would not receive the offsetting credit for as many at 18 months after paying their bill with the education institution, and perhaps as much as two years after committing to attend a given academic program.

Of course, taxpayers with sufficient positive tax liability to adjust their income tax withholding over the course of the year may be able to receive at least part of their expected credit during the same tax year that the expense is incurred. In contrast, taxpayers with no tax liability, that is those receiving a refundable credit, cannot adjust their withholding below zero, and therefore cannot receive their credit prior to filing a return. As a result, the lag between paying tuition and receipt of the tax credit described in the preceding paragraph predominantly affects taxpayers with low and moderate incomes. It has been suggested by Lochner and Monge-Naranjo and others that this delay can create a barrier to entry for students who are cash constrained, or otherwise hesitant to incur an obligation against future tax credits.[53] Even for those not constrained, the long lag could lessen any incentive effect of the credit on enrollment.

Advanced refundability of the AOTC is occasionally proposed as a way to alleviate these problems because it could make credit funds available to students closer to the time when the money was actually spent. The money could either be distributed to the student/taxpayer, or remitted directly to the education institution. Taxpayers would reconcile the advanced credit with their eligible credit amount in their subsequent income tax return filings. They would repay amounts provided for which they were ultimately not eligible, or receive additional credits for

---

[52] The credit begins to phase out at $80,000.
[53] Ellwood and Kane (2000) argue that credit constraints may impede enrollment for some students. Lochner and Monge-Naranjo (2008) show document a strong relationship between family wealth and income and college attendance and show that this is consistent with binding credit constraints. Belley and Lochner (2007) present evidence suggesting the constraints may have become more important in recent years. In contrast, Nielsen, Sorensen and Taber (2008) and Cameron and Taber (2004) provide evidence that short-term constraints have little impact on education outcomes.

eligible amounts not claimed in advance. To minimize repayments, the advance amount could be limited to a share of the entire credit or a share of the estimated credit for which the taxpayer is eligible. Thus, advance refundability would not affect the amount of the credit for which the student was ultimately eligible to claim.

Advance refundability of the AOTC would only, by definition, apply to students attending at least half time. Although many of these students would face gross tuition amounts far in excess of the value of the tax credits, many others, particularly those attending community college or other low cost institutions would be considering attendance at programs for which the credit would cover a large share of their tuition costs.

1. The Argument in Favor of Advance Refundability:

Some potential students interested in furthering their educations may be cash constrained. These students might be unable to enroll even though the resources are expected to be available in the future. Providing access to the funds at the time they are needed would eliminate a barrier to enrollment while improving incentives for some to obtain additional education. Furthermore, asking students to borrow against future tax payments is an inefficient use of student resources, and if the student relies on subsidized loans, an inefficient way to use government funds.

2. The Arguments Against Advance Refundability:

Although there are many good arguments for improving the coordination of expected Federal assistance with tuition payment dates, it is unclear that advance refundability of the AOTC could be administered efficiently.

Administering Advance Refundability Would Require Duplicate Needs Analysis and Administration: Many of the individuals eligible for an AOTC (and particularly a refundable AOTC) will have filled out a FAFSA and therefore, the Department of Education will already have a fairly accurate assessment of the applicant's resources using prior year tax data. Moreover, financial aid administrators also have some limited discretion to take other factors into consideration (such as the refusal of a non-custodial parent to contribute to a child's education) when making an aid award. An advance refundable tax credit would be duplicative, and would likely never be as effective as existing Department of Education programs at targeting aid to the low-income population.

As seen in Table 7, the low-income population receiving the refundable AOTC is largely the same population receiving the Pell grant. This population would be better served by an additional outlay program such as that described in Option 5 above (the AOTC-Pell Boost). Such a program would achieve the goal of providing funds in a timely manner without requiring the student to submit to a second set of procedures, including reconciliation, to ensure that the student is in compliance with the law.

It has been suggested that the FAFSA process is burdensome relative to filing for a tax credit, and that advanced refundability would provide timely aid with less effort on the part of the student. While the FAFSA can be daunting, much of the relative simplicity in obtaining an education credit would disappear if the credit amount were advanced and then reconciled at a later date. The Department of Education in conjunction with IRS has also made progress on simplifying the FAFSA.[54]

Advance Refundability is Complex: Advance refundability would be administratively challenging and potentially expensive. The IRS or some other entity would need to estimate who was likely to be eligible to receive the credit prior to the end of the tax year. The IRS would need to issue payments on a rolling basis as individuals made decisions to enroll in a vast array of programs with different start dates and tuition rates, at a wide range of institutions that may vary in their ability to participate in administering the payments, if required. A much more precise analog to the 1098-T would need to be developed so that the IRS could track spending, ensure compliance, and issue funds in a timely way. The 1098-T is currently issued once a year based on data available at a given point in time, and is insufficient to support the implementation of advance refundability.

---

[54] These efforts are documented in U.S. Department of Education (2009), R_eport to Congress on Efforts to Simplify the Free Application for Federal Student Aid (FAFSA)._

Additionally, the IRS would be required to develop procedures for the distribution of the advanced funds. Options would range from mailing checks to the individuals to advancing the funds to the education institutions and integrating the advanced amounts into the student's financial aid packages.

Advance Refundability is Expensive: First, IRS would face direct costs associated with distributing the money and issuing checks to individuals or institutions. Second, the administration of advance refundability would require new procedures for the reconciliation of funds distributed with the funds for which the person was actually eligible at the end of the tax year. Depending on the nature of the advanceable program, advance refundability of the AOTC could involve reconciling millions of returns and issuing millions of checks. Taxpayers might be asked to repay advanced funds in some cases, which could create hardships for some. Any provision to hold harmless those taxpayers whose circumstances changed would increase program costs. Fear of a repayment obligation could limit the appeal of the program. Furthermore, the IRS would need to integrate this new program into existing processing and enforcement programs. Treasury expects that advanced refundability of the AOTC would increase noncompliance, partially due to the increased complexity of the credit. Moreover, if the refunded amounts were relatively small compared to audit thresholds, it is possible that much of the noncompliance would go unchallenged.

3. Past and Future Experience with Advanceable Credits

To date, Federal experience with advanceable credits has been limited. The two main advanceable credits are the Health Coverage Tax Credit (HCTC), which pays a large share of health insurance premium costs for certain qualified displaced workers, and the advance payment of the Earned Income Tax Credit (EITC), which prior to repeal allowed eligible taxpayers with children to receive up to sixty percent of their EITC in their regular paychecks. The HCTC has several administrative requirements to determine eligibility and premiums for a very small population of participants, and is therefore not a good model to use as a design for expanding to larger populations.[55] The advance payment option for the EITC was unpopular with taxpayers even though evidence suggests that many eligible households are cash constrained during the year. The reasons for low utilization are not fully understood but may include lack of awareness, preference for lump sum payments, fear of being forced to make a sizable payment to the IRS if circumstances change, and distaste for discussing participation in a tax credit program with their employers. IRS efforts over the years to improve participation through outreach were not successful. At the time of repeal, around one percent of the eligible were participating.[56]

Public laws 111-148 and 111-152, collectively referred to as the Affordable Care Act (ACA), provide for a refundable tax credit for health insurance coverage purchased through a federal or state exchange. Notably, the health insurance market does not currently have a widely available and large-scale grant program analogous to the Pell Grant to help low-income families purchase health care. Thus, it was necessary to create a new mechanism for enrolling families in insurance coverage and delivering subsidies at the time that they are paying for health insurance. Health insurance exchanges will use the most recent available tax data, along with other more recent information, to determine an advance payment. The exchange will enroll an individual in a plan of their choosing and the Treasury will send payment directly to the insurer. At the end of the year, individuals will be required to reconcile their advance payments on their tax returns. Individuals who receive an advance payment that exceeds the end-of-the-year tax credit amount will be required to pay back the difference up to a limit, while those who receive an advance payment that is less than the end-of-the year credit will be able to claim the full difference.

IX. Volunteer Service Requirement as a Condition of AOTC Eligibility

The American Recovery and Reinvestment Act of 2009 (ARRA) calls for the Secretary of the Treasury and the Secretary of Education to investigate the feasibility of implementing a requirement to fulfill a volunteer obligation in order to be eligible to receive this credit. This

---

[55] Administrative hurdles to management are described in GAO (2004).

[56] Participation and noncompliance are described in GAO (2007). IRS efforts to increase awareness are described in IRS (1999).

section provides an analysis of what the requirement could mean to the relevant stakeholders: the students who would perform the community service; the taxpayers who may claim the credit on behalf of the student; the educational institution the student may attend; the Internal Revenue Service, which administers all tax provisions; and the local charitable organizations at which the students would volunteer.

The law mandating the study does not specify the characteristics of the service requirement, including the nature of the volunteer obligation, the relationship between the volunteer obligation and the resulting benefits (for example, if the recipient of a relatively small AOTC would have the same obligation as student receiving the maximum AOTC), how it would be administered (for example, if students could self-report, or if the reporting would be done by the charity or by the institution attended by the student), or any other characteristics of the requirement. Therefore this section begins by outlining the components that a service requirement might entail. The section continues with a description of some of the challenges to successful implementation of a service requirement within a tax credit. This includes consideration of the potential impact of a service requirement on tax compliance and on the effectiveness of education tax credits at supporting families with education expenses. For this analysis, it is generally assumed that the credit would only apply to the AOTC, and not the LLC, although some discussion about the variation in the size of the credit is included.

As part of preparing this report, Treasury requested public comment on the requirement and what it would mean to stakeholders. Treasury received more than sixty responses, many of which were extremely thoughtful and insightful. High-quality analyses were received from groups representing universities, researchers, the service learning community, and from taxpayers. Their comments are integrated throughout the text and then presented in detail in a separate section toward the end of the discussion. With few exceptions, the respondents were overwhelmingly opposed to a volunteer service requirement.

A. A Framework of a Volunteer Requirement

Any proposal to add a volunteer requirement for receipt of an education tax credit would likely contain the six components described below. Within this framework, there is a great deal of flexibility about the level of oversight, the level of engagement by students, and the purpose of the credit. Although it is easiest to think of the administration of a complex program by a university or other large institution, it is important to remember that the requirement would also apply to students at small technical schools and at for-profit institutions, both of which cater to a less traditional student population. The six components are as follows:

1. Definition of a legitimate program. Criteria would be established that define a legitimate volunteer program and legitimate activity.

2. Students self-identify and choose to participate. Students would self-identify that they are likely to be eligible for a tax credit based on the estimated income and education expenses,[57] and decide to pursue a volunteer opportunity.

3. Students and volunteer opportunities are matched. The nature of the match is part of the program design. For example, students could be required to find volunteer opportunities on their own, work in conjunction with an office within the university (or other educational institution), or coordinate with a charity-based office. It could be that educational institutions are mandated to ensure that sufficient legitimate opportunities exist for all students (through outreach and coordination), or the responsibility for finding a valid opportunity could reside elsewhere.

4. Students perform the community service, presumably to the satisfaction of the charity.

---

[57] Income means income on the tax return; thus, for dependent students, this would be income on their parent's return and for individuals paying for their own education, or the education of their spouse, this would be income as it appears on the individual's own return. Furthermore, education expenses would be net of grant or scholarship aid as defined in the tax code.

5. <u>Completion is reported and taxes returns are filed.</u> Reporting requirements must also be part of the credit design. The nature of the reporting could be through the educational institution (perhaps on a redesigned 1098-T), by the student or the taxpayer claiming the student (perhaps simply self-reported), by the charitable organization (perhaps on an additional information return), or by multiple parties.

6. <u>IRS processes returns,</u> which would include conducting enforcement activities.

The purpose of presenting a barebones framework is to ensure that the following discussion covers all major implementation challenges and is sufficiently focused on the integration of all parties. Establishing a requirement is certainly possible, but it is less obvious that sufficient safeguards could be created as part of the requirement to ensure access to opportunities, accountability, and a valuable experience to the students and charities involved. It is also not obvious that IRS could administer a meaningful requirement in a manner that is consistent with IRS's primary mission to administer the tax system and that meets reasonable standards of compliance and efficiency.

B. Challenges:

1. <u>Definition of a legitimate program:</u>

Successful administration of a volunteer requirement depends on a shared understanding of the program's rules and procedures by the main stakeholders: taxpayers and volunteers, the organizations that accept the services of the volunteers, and the education institutions the volunteers attend. It is not the purpose of this report to establish policy goals or to construct a vision statement in support of such goals. However, without a well-articulated statement of these policy goals, analysts will not be able to establish criteria for judging the success of the program or its cost efficiency.

On a more fundamental level, defining a program requires articulating the kinds of activities that would be permissible and not permissible. It would be necessary to develop criteria that would mandate the minimal effort level required for receipt of the credit. Linking a single day's charitable activity to receipt of a $2,500 credit may belittle the charitable effort and would not warrant the infrastructure required for administration of this credit. On the other hand, a requirement that is too burdensome would discourage participation by students who may find it more efficient to increase their hours of paid employment and forego the credit. Not all students receive the full credit, which suggests that some prorating of the required effort level may be appropriate. Criteria would also be necessary to determine which organizations would be considered valid for credit purposes. Should the list be restricted to public charities, or should individuals be able to meet the requirement at religious organizations, political organizations, sports organizations, or other groups of their own choosing? If the requirement were to be administered by the educational institutions, should these institutions be required to accept activities that may be in opposition to the charters of their institution? Policies at existing volunteer programs and service learning programs (such as AmeriCorps[58] and those affiliated with Campus Compact[59]) may provide some insight into how many of these questions should be answered. However, establishing a program of this magnitude (100 times larger than AmeriCorps) that also integrates the procedures and policies governing tax administration will require unique and creative solutions.

2. Students self-identify and choose to participate

Education credits are received by taxpayers as part of the ordinary tax filing process after the close of the year. The actual volunteer effort would occur prior to the end of the tax year, thus largely before annual income is known to the taxpayer. Many, but not all taxpayers can safely predict whether or not they will be income-eligible for the full credit, but others cannot due to the phase-out of the credit beginning at $80,000 ($160,000 for joint filers) or due to the phase-in of the nonrefundable piece of the credit (which is dependent on income tax liability).

---

[58] AmeriCorps operates two programs that place individuals in community service positions, pay a stipend, and upon completion of the program, a college scholarship. The website is at http://www.americorps.gov/.
[59] Campus Compact is "a coalition of University presidents committed to promoting service learning opportunities on campus." The website is at http://www.compact.org/.

It may also be the case, particularly in the first years after enactment, that students and families might not know about the additional requirement for receipt of the credit. To ensure awareness of the requirement by students and their families, the education institutions and IRS would need to conduct outreach well before the end of the tax year. Furthermore, because a large share of the student population in any given year is new to the AOTC, and thus, would be new to any volunteer requirement, the necessity for at least some outreach would always be present.

Some students who qualify for an AOTC under existing rules may opt out of completing the volunteer requirement or be unable to complete the volunteer requirement, thereby forfeiting up to $2,500 of federal aid per year.[60] Comments from respondents and the Community College League of California (2004) suggest that those who would struggle hardest to fulfill the requirement, and thus maintain eligibility for the assistance, would be those with the fewest resources, particularly those with large commitments outside the classroom.[61] This potential outcome would be in conflict with the Administration's dual goal of making college more affordable and increasing access.[62]

3.   Students and volunteer opportunities are matched.

Establishing criteria for how willing students and volunteer opportunities would be matched is an important feature of the program design. Challenges to consider include ensuring that sufficient legitimate opportunities exist in a given region for all students who are potentially eligible and interested in participating, and ensuring that the new credit does not undermine existing programs. Representatives from the service learning community described the ongoing challenges faced by their institutions in creating opportunities, and in nurturing the personal relationships developed between the staff at local charities and their institutions. Respondents from rural programs highlighted the lack of local infrastructure, and sometimes the limited need for volunteers. Large state universities may have tens of thousands of students but be located in

---

[60] Many but not all of these students would have been eligible for the smaller tuition deduction or lifetime learning credit.

[61] Those most likely to be affected are students with dependents, students who work more than 20 hours per week, and students who do not have access to transportation.

[62] See http://www.whitehouse.gov/blog/2010/10/13/american-opportunity-tax-credit-and-presidents-event-today and http://www.whitehouse.gov/blog/2011/03/23/call-action-college-completion.

small communities far from a population center.[63] A 2003 study of 21 "high quality" volunteer programs found that more than half of their study participants indicated that they did not need more volunteers, and the remaining nine had specific skill and scheduling requirements.[64] These challenges to assuring that sufficient positions exist are exacerbated once we consider that many students would be unable to perform their required service during normal business hours due to the nature of their academic programs (nursing students and others in highly structured training programs would be in class most days), and additional responsibilities (most students have jobs, and non-traditional students may have family commitments).

If the matching is done informally by students, such that each student seeks out a suitable volunteer requirement on his or her own, success for some students may be limited by their youth and inexperience. It is not clear what fairness concerns would dictate for students who made a legitimate effort to fulfill the requirement but were unable to do so due to insufficient opportunities or insufficient job-seeking skills, and how these students could be distinguished from those whose failure to fulfill the requirement may be less sympathetic.

If instead the matching were done in conjunction with an office within the education institution, by the government, or through cooperation among the non-profits, questions regarding how these responsibilities should be funded would arise. Should these costs be borne by the charities that presumably would benefit from the community service provided? Should these costs instead be absorbed by the education institutions? What is the appropriate level of responsibility for the education institutions, particularly those that are small or for-profit?

4. Students perform the community service.

Although this portion of the framework would seem straightforward, there may be compliance issues to resolve in certain cases. The earlier discussion suggests that this requirement should represent a non-trivial time commitment. Thus it should be expected that some individuals

___

[63] For example, the main campus of the University of Connecticut has 16,000 undergraduates and is located in a town of fewer than 11,000 people (some of the 11,000 represents students who live in the community).
[64] See the *Grantmaker Forum on Community and National Service* (2003).

would fail to fulfill their obligations. Ensuring only entitled students received the credit may be challenging. For example, it would seem likely that some students would volunteer at an organization assisting a community to which the student belongs. For example, students may volunteer in programs affiliated with their own house of worship or at a youth organization in their home town. In these cases, the relationship between the organization and the student and between the organization and the student's parent (the taxpayer) may be long-established and close. It is likely that the charities would feel pressure to "check off" that the obligation was completed even if the student did not do so – pressure may be particularly intense if it were perceived that the student's parent would "lose" the aid. Commenters expressed some concern about the potential subjectivity of any standard of completion.

Other issues involve the costs and risks to the organization of accepting volunteers, particularly if accepted in great number. Charities could incur costs in many areas: increased security and asset protection, background checks, training and oversight, construction of appropriate projects for the volunteers that may not be the best use of the manager's time, and recordkeeping. One respondent described the large variation in the assets (and liabilities) that her volunteers bring, which dictates the level of oversight required and the objective value of the volunteer's time to her organization. At least some charities may find that these costs exceed the potential benefits from accepting AOTC volunteers and decline to participate.

   5.   Completion is reported and tax returns are filed.

A volunteer requirement could be designed with either minimal or very precise reporting requirements. At a minimum, taxpayers could be asked to self-report to the IRS that they have fulfilled the requirement, perhaps as a check-box on their return. This minimal level of reporting would be the easiest for IRS to administer, but is likely to lead to noncompliance which would undermine the legitimacy of the requirement. Another option would be augment the check-box with additional reporting on the Form 1098-T, which is already issued to most students. The education institutions could be required to determine if the requirement was completed before issuing Form 1098-T, but this would impose burdens on these institutions, and potentially insert the institution's financial aid office into a relationship outside the normal purview. A third option would be to create an additional reporting mechanism, a new Form 1098, for the charities to fill out and submit. It is well-known that taxpayer compliance improves when there is reliable third-party reporting, but increasing reporting must only be considered after an evaluation of the burden it would impose, and if a sufficiently high level of accuracy can be expected from those who report.

6. IRS processes returns, which would include conducting enforcement activities.

Discussions were held with IRS regarding the potential IRS role in administering this requirement. IRS stressed that the IRS is first and foremost a tax administration agency, and should therefore not have a role in making subjective determinations regarding satisfactory completion of a volunteer requirement. For the same reasons, the IRS should not manage the commitment and certification process.

If additional information were included on a revised Form 1098-T, or even a new form, the IRS would be able to process the returns in a manner similar to the processing of other provisions, but serious challenges to successful and efficient processing would exist. Challenges include timing, noncompliance, and additional resource cost.

Timing: Matching of information returns with tax return data can take twelve to eighteen months. Thus, the main enforcement tool available to the IRS would be an audit conducted well after the return claiming the benefit has been filed.

Furthermore, for the IRS to administer this credit, it would need to be on a tax year calendar like other income tax provisions and not on an academic calendar. This mismatch between the calendars of academia and the IRS could create challenges for students who would have very limited time to complete a requirement recognized by their university, and would put pressure on Form 1098-T processing by the institutions (if required to administer the requirement).

Specifically, the tax year for individuals begins in January and finishes at the end of December. In contrast, for most students, the academic year begins with the fall semester in August or

September and continues through the following summer. New students would have only three or four months left in the tax year in which to find a placement and complete the volunteering for that year. The education institution would also be rushed. Currently, the education institution mails the 1098-T to students in the January following the end of a tax year. The 1098-T contains billing information from the first part of the current academic year, and the last part of the previous academic year. Education institutions have most of the fall to fill out the 1098-T and transmit the information to the students and the IRS because in most cases, the amounts on the 1098-T will be known relatively early in the fall semester, if not before. If a volunteer requirement were put in place, students might still be working on their required volunteer effort throughout the fall semester, (returning students may have completed the requirement in the previous academic year (but still in this tax year), new students would most likely not have had this opportunity), but the January deadline for sending the Form 1098-T could not be pushed back. This, in turn would put pressure on Form 1098-T processing by the institutions.

Noncompliance: Noncompliance with the rules governing education credits has been discussed in an earlier section along with details about the limitations of the Form 1098-T. Adding an additional requirement, particularly one with as many complications as this one, is likely to increase noncompliance because it creates an additional restriction on eligibility[65]. Presumably adding this requirement would create the need for a larger compliance presence in this area, with the associated costs.

Resource Cost: IRS would face a number of costs to implementing a volunteer requirement. These include those related to the following: a) modification of the Form 1098-T or creation of a new form, b) integration of the new or modified form in the IRS' electronic filing systems, and transcription costs for those returns that are submitted on paper, c) the processing and storing of additional data, d) the matching of additional data elements during processing, and e) conducting outreach and answering taxpayer questions about the requirement. Furthermore, since it is expected there would be a substantial amount of noncompliance, IRS would face costs related to improving fraud detection systems, and the general increased compliance presence.

---

[65] For example, some individuals who may be compliant under current law might continue claiming the credit without legitimately fulfilling the volunteer service requirement.

The preceding two sections have identified key challenges in designing and administering a volunteer service requirement within a tax credit and demonstrated that although it may be feasible to add a requirement of this nature to the existing AOTC, it is most likely not feasible to do it in a way that would be consistent with good tax policy. A volunteer requirement would be burdensome to the institutions administering the credit, be burdensome to students and taxpayers, lead to noncompliance by taxpayers and charities, and increase IRS administrative costs. Furthermore, it is not clear that such a requirement would actually achieve the likely policy goals of increasing civic engagement or increasing resources available to the charities.

C. Public Comment:

In connection with this study, Treasury solicited public comments on the feasibility of implementing a volunteer requirement.[66] The following questions were asked:

1. Should students be required to fulfill a community service requirement for receipt of an education credit? Why or why not?

2. If there were a community service requirement, should the institutions providing post-secondary education and training (hereafter, colleges) be required to administer it? Please elaborate.

3. If there were a community service requirement, and the colleges were required to administer the requirement, what would be the main operational and administrative challenges the schools would face in implementing this requirement? Topics to address include, but are not limited to:
   a. How would colleges ensure that there are meaningful community service opportunities available for all students?

---

[66] Notice 2010-7021, released on Tuesday, March 30, 2010 is found on page 15772 of the Federal Register, vol 75, No.60, at http://edocket.access.gpo.gov/2010/pdf/2010-7021.pdf.

b. How would colleges ensure that eligible students are identified and able to claim the credit while students who failed to fulfill the community service requirement are not able to claim the credit?

c. How could existing infrastructure on campuses help or hinder the implementation of this requirement?

d. If administration of this credit involved additional reporting, perhaps on a revised IRS Form 1098-T or were tied to the campus-based work study program, how would institutions be affected?

4. What challenges would students face in fulfilling this community service requirement if it were adopted?

A total of 62 responses were received from a variety of stakeholders. Most responses were provided by university staff, including professors, program managers, deans, and representatives from financial aid offices. They represented the full range of institutions, including elite colleges, state universities, community colleges, and trade schools. Additional responses were received from trade associations and other consortia representing university interests in general and community service interests specifically. Ten responses were received from private citizens, most of whom had experience supporting a student or paying for their own educations. Finally, one response was received representing tax preparers. In addition to these responses, interviews were conducted with representatives from one non-profit and with educators and administrators involved with service learning.[67]

All but four respondents were strongly opposed to requiring a volunteer commitment for receipt of the federal education credits, though the majority of respondents also stated that encouraging volunteerism was an important policy goal. Very few thought that the requirement should be

---

[67] Service learning programs are academic programs or classes that integrate a volunteer or community service component into the curriculum, along with assessment tools and writing assignments. Critical to the successful implementation of the programs is an ongoing relationship between the volunteer organizations where the students serve and the teachers, professors, and administrators in the education institutions attended by the students. More information about service learning is available from the National Service Learning Clearinghouse at http://www.servicelearning.org/what-service-learning.

administered by the universities,[68] which is consistent with the fact that this sector provided most of the responses.

Question 1 – Should There Be a Voluntary Service Requirement?

The overwhelming majority of respondents thought that requiring a volunteer commitment for receipt of federal education credits was undesirable even though most also stated that encouraging volunteerism was a legitimate policy goal. The two responses in support of a service requirement were brief: one stressed the importance of giving back, and the second described the potential for the credit to increase the visibility of local charities. Two respondents were ambivalent: they were not opposed to the idea of a requirement in principle, but were concerned that in practice the credit would be unadministrable or too burdensome to students. Those in opposition provided more detail. Their reasons for opposing the credit varied and are presented thematically below.

It Isn't Volunteering. Many respondents opened with strong statements about the nature of volunteerism, and how the relationship between donor and donee no longer holds once the activity is required. Respondents described a requirement as "forced volunteering," a "paradox" or "not community service at all." Two respondents likened the requirement to slavery. Others provided more subtle arguments on how requiring the service could change the quality of the work effort (and thereby diminish the benefit to the charities for whom the work was done), or the attitude of the volunteers (who might become less likely to volunteer again in the future).

A Service Obligation Is Inconsistent with the Purpose of the Credits. Some respondents opened their comments by reiterating the purpose of the existing credits, which is to assist families with education expenses and thereby encourage attendance and persistence. In support of their position, they made reference to the original discussions in the 1990's by Congress and the Clinton administration that surrounded the education credits' introduction. These respondents stated that other goals (such as encouraging a deeper connection to society or increasing

---

[68] Most respondents referred to universities, and not educational institutions in their comments, although some respondents did come from smaller institutions.

assistance available to local charities) may have merit, but because these goals are inconsistent with the stated purpose of the credits, they should not be linked to receipt of the credits. Respondents writing on this theme further stressed that the volunteer service requirement would make it more difficult for students to claim the credits and thereby weaken any positive impact the credits could have on attendance or persistence.

The Requirement Would Add Complexity. Respondents noted that the existing education credits are already very complicated, with many individuals "leaving money on the table" due to this complexity. Additional rules and requirements would exacerbate this situation and undermine the administration's goal of increasing access to higher education. As an example, respondents described individuals who would not know that they were potentially eligible for a credit or know the size of their credit until after the tax year is over and their income is determined. At this point, however, it would be too late for such individuals to do any required volunteering. Other respondents stated that the purpose of the Internal Revenue Service is to administer the collection of taxes; administering a volunteer service requirement would be different from most everything else the IRS does and outside the IRS' area of expertise. The respondents were concerned that this requirement would put IRS in the position of making value judgments about taxpayer behavior and recommended that IRS responsibilities remain restricted to its central mission of collecting taxes.

A Volunteer Service Requirement Would Be Unfair. Some respondents noted that the challenge of fulfilling any volunteer service requirement would be greater for some students than for others and the most affluent students would face no volunteer requirement at all. The unequal burden struck these respondents as unfair. These respondents reminded Treasury to consider the large number of non-traditional students, disabled students, students in trade schools, and those who might have too many additional responsibilities to complete the volunteer requirement; such students could be forced to opt out of the tuition assistance. A responding professor stated that his work shows that those most likely to fulfill a volunteer requirement, and thus receive the assistance, would be those in the more affluent portion of the credit-eligible population. Additional respondents noted that not all students would have equal access to suitable volunteer opportunities due to the resources and locations of the schools they attend, and the characteristics of their academic programs. For example, some students attend universities with well-established volunteer programs in areas of the country where many non-profits are active. Other students attend smaller programs without these resources and opportunities. For example, one respondent compared the resources at a large university to those at her small-town beauty school. Some students do not have cars and would have limited access to off-campus opportunities. Some students, including nursing students, attend tightly structured programs that may include on-site training during much of the workday. Students in these programs would find fulfilling a volunteer requirement much harder than students in more flexible programs. Some students are disabled, or have children of their own. Respondents worried that overall, those who would struggle the most to fulfill the requirement would be those with the fewest resources. As stated by one respondent, from this perspective, the volunteer requirement is potentially regressive.

There Are Insufficient Meaningful Opportunities Available for Students. Many respondents stated that there would most likely be insufficient opportunities in some locations for students to fulfill this requirement even if intentions were good. Respondents noted that many American universities and colleges are in rural areas. Local charities in these areas would not have the infrastructure to provide opportunities to the large population of students needing to fulfill the requirement. Matching students with opportunities, particularly students who do not have transportation, have disabilities, or have limited opportunities to perform the service during normal business hours would be challenging, if not impossible.

The Benefits to Charities are Mixed. Respondents provided insightful comments on the effect this requirement would have on the charities receiving the volunteers. Naturally, the number of volunteers available to many charities would increase if a volunteer requirement was mandated, and a larger pool could be advantageous to charities struggling to meet their charitable goals. However, it was not clear to those responding that the benefits from increasing the volunteer pool in this way would be sufficient to induce the charities and community organizations to absorb the influx of students. Integrating new volunteers imposes certain direct costs on the charities. Costs cited include those related to providing additional training to volunteers and staff, conducting background checks, providing supervision and oversight of volunteers, and increasing exposure to risk and liability. In addition, there would be administrative costs to managing the volunteers, including the costs of hiring additional staff, and completing any reporting requirements.

It was also suggested that charities might be pressured to increase their volunteer programs to absorb the influx of students, which could detract from their mission. One respondent suggested that the placement and oversight might simply "overwhelm" the agencies, and leave them spending more of their limited time and resources on administrative duties, rather than serving the populations who need their assistance. Another respondent echoed these concerns when describing her own experience with volunteer workers. This respondent's organization, like many other charitable organizations, "hires" teen volunteers from within the community served. Although some volunteers were excellent, others were less able -- creating meaningful volunteer opportunities for these teens is a challenging and often time-consuming process.

There was one dissenting opinion on this topic presented by a respondent favoring a volunteer requirement. This respondent thought that charities would benefit. He described his experience with a Disney-based incentive program – Disneyland provided free tickets to individuals who showed that they had done some recent volunteering. This respondent was pleased with the influx of volunteers his organization witnessed as a result of Disney's program, and credited this influx with increasing local awareness about the charity he serves.

A Requirement could affect Existing Opportunities. Many respondents wrote at length about the value of community service – to the charities served, to the wider community, and to the individuals who volunteer – and the importance of encouraging individuals to engage in their community at all stages of their life. However, as described above, the majority of the respondents doubted that a tuition tax credit was a sensible way to achieve this goal. They argued that a tuition tax credit was too narrow because it only targeted credit-eligible students and not potential volunteers at other stages of life or for whom a tuition credit is otherwise irrelevant. Respondents described existing campus-based community service programs (e.g., service learning opportunities, AmeriCorps, and the Federal Work-Study Program[69]) and suggested that government resources would be better spent on providing additional support to these programs than on creating the infrastructure for a tuition credit program. Respondents wrote that in many cases, the administrators of the existing programs have already developed ties to local organizations for student placement, and have extensive knowledge about local needs. As described by the respondents (some representing these programs), these programs are very successful and should be encouraged. Respondents expressed concerns, however, that a volunteer requirement would divert limited resources away from these programs as education institutions felt pressure to accommodate the credit-seeking students at the expense of students in other programs.

Question 2 - Credit Administration: Should the Schools do it?

Most respondents were opposed to the schools administering any volunteer requirement. This result was not completely unexpected because nearly all of the respondents were school administrators or otherwise connected to higher education. They had two main reasons for their opposition, which are discussed below.

Inappropriate Role for the Schools. First, many respondents thought it was inappropriate for the schools to be involved in a "discussion" between the taxpayer and the IRS (beyond potentially reporting dollar amounts). Respondents commenting on this were particularly opposed to a university role in assessing the legitimacy of any particular volunteer activity and stated that this kind of role occurs nowhere else in the tax code. Respondents suggested that university administration would mean that universities were assigned an enforcement role regarding the

---

[69] Representatives from each of these programs were among the respondents. Descriptions of these programs are available at the following locations. Campus Compact is "a coalition of University presidents committed to promoting service learning opportunities on campus." The website is at http://www.compact.org/. AmeriCorps operates two programs that place individuals in community service positions, pay a stipend, and upon completion of the program, a college scholarship. The website is at http://www.americorps.gov/. The Federal Work-Study Program provides federally subsidized employment opportunities for income-eligible students. To meet program requirements, at least seven percent of the work-study students at a given institution should be employed in community service positions, although not all universities are able to achieve this level. More information is available at http://www2.ed.gov/programs/fws/index.html. All URLs were last accessed on June 10, 2011.

assessment of an individual's tax liability – a role that the respondents felt should belong to the IRS alone. These respondents generally distinguished information reporting, as on the current Form 1098-T, from assessments of whether a student's experience met credit requirements. In general, the respondents presented few complaints about existing information reporting (although many stressed that it was time-consuming and burdensome), but worried about being asked to take on a more normative role that would include determining which volunteer placements qualified, tracking student attendance, and then later verifying that service was completed. Respondents also expressed concern that administration of the credits by the universities would ultimately lead to the exclusion of legitimate volunteer opportunities from credit eligibility because these opportunities were outside the university's awareness.

University Administration would be Expensive and Unfunded. Second, the respondents objected to the expense – they viewed the requirement as an unfunded mandate and argued that the bulk of the additional responsibilities would fall heaviest on offices that have recently faced staffing cuts. Many suggested that the requirement, if administered by the schools, could lead to increased fees and tuition. Respondents from university registrar and financial aid offices described current staffing shortages and the long list of existing responsibilities. Some of the respondents representing small institutions noted that their "office of financial aid" is generally one person with limited experience. These respondents questioned if their institutions would be able to do a sufficiently good job administering this credit and were concerned that their limitations would harm their students.

Alternatives to University Administration. Very few respondents suggested alternatives to university-based administration. In general, these respondents saw a qualitative difference between tax-based aid and university- or Department of Education-based aid. Most of these respondents suggested that since the volunteer requirement was tax-based, information should be reported directly by the taxpayer, perhaps in conjunction with information reporting by the charitable organizations.

Question 3 – Main Operational and Administrative Challenges.

Challenges to the Universities. As described by the respondents, one of the main challenges to the successful implementation of a meaningful community service opportunity would be ensuring that sufficient opportunities exist, and that there was a reasonable match between these opportunities and the needs and limitations of the credit-eligible students. Respondents who addressed this issue did not believe that there would be sufficient opportunities in all communities for all students who would be potentially eligible to receive a credit and wanted to volunteer. As an example, they highlighted the difficulties that some institutions have meeting existing service requirements for the Federal Work-Study Program (Title IV).[70] At least two responses were submitted on behalf of institutions that do not participate in Title IV – these respondents suggested that their institutions might have even fewer connections to the local non-profit community than participating institutions. To highlight the expected problem with finding opportunities, one respondent cited the statistic that the number of students who would potentially be eligible for an education credit is bigger by an order of magnitude than those participating in "work-study".

As reported above, many respondents stated that limited opportunity would be a particular challenge to students at rural institutions, although this is where many academic institutions are located. Local charities in these areas would not have the infrastructure to provide opportunities to the large population of students, and existing community need might not correspond with student availability. Respondents from the service learning community gave examples of challenges faced by their programs with developing and maintaining relationships with local charities. In particular, one respondent described a program that pulled back from its original goals because the relationships could not be sustained.

---

[70] 3,400 institutions participate in the Federal Work-Study program (Title IV). This program provides funds to help support students with financial need through part-time employment. As a requirement of the program, at least seven percent of the funds must go to students engaged in community service positions off campus, and at least one student must be employed as a reading tutor. Institutions that find it difficult to achieve the seven percent level may apply for a waiver. Small and rural institutions are most likely to find it onerous to achieve the seven percent requirement.

Respondents agreed that it would be important to ensure that only students who fulfill the requirements should receive the credit. Respondents were less sure that the institutions they represent would have the resources to do this. For example, the respondents expected that financial aid offices would have the responsibility for administering the credit. This office typically has limited resources, and no history of doing anything like this. Some suggested that charities might feel pressured, as might the schools, to sign off that community service was completed without proper documentation, particularly if the volunteers came from the communities benefitting from the service.

Other respondents focused on the word "meaningful." All agreed, perhaps tautologically, that the requirement must be meaningful, but the definitions of meaningful ranged from a "few hours self-reported" to multiple hours per year across the term. Respondents foresaw challenges in choosing the appropriate obligation, but were unsure how to evaluate what the appropriate metric would be for measuring meaningful participation, particularly if the obligation varied with expected credit size. Hours were considered an imperfect measure, and auditing of the charities would clearly be administratively burdensome. Respondents were not comfortable with being the arbiter of "meaningful" and suggested there would be a lack of consensus.

Campuses have four pieces of infrastructure identified as being helpful in administrating the requirements: three existing programs (the Federal Work-Study Program, AmeriCorps and campus service learning programs), and financial aid offices. Respondents suggested that it would be challenging to expand the programs, as might be required if a volunteer obligation was imposed. Particularly in the case of service learning, the volunteer programs are small, intense, and not easily expandable. Respondents questioned if programs could survive massive growth or, if the programs ran in parallel, if the volunteer opportunities cultivated by service learning offices for their programs and courses would go to "credit students," thus crowding out the opportunities for their clientele. In a world of limited opportunities, respondents questioned how one would choose among students for participation. Would these programs survive an influx of the less-committed? Respondents expressed concern that this requirement would undermine their hard work that created service learning programs. Respondents feared that competition for a limited number of spots, the influx of the less-committed, and being asked to potentially rank students based on need would undermine the well-documented successes of service learning.

Reporting Challenges to the Universities: Institutions felt that they could do a "check the box" along the lines of the existing 1098-T, but were unenthusiastic about accepting responsibility for making sure that this box did more than report that the "student waved a form at us from some charity."

Question 4 - Challenges to students.

One approach to matching students to volunteer opportunities would be to rely on the students to conduct the match. Many responding universities questioned whether some students could find sufficient legitimate opportunities on their own. A few pointed out that it would be challenging for some to identify opportunities because of their youth and naïveté. Others noted the challenge when there are not enough volunteer opportunities around. The university respondents thought that this approach would be less challenging than university administration, but completing the requirement would be less attainable for some students than it would be if there were more oversight.

Other respondents pointed out that the requirement would be far easier to fulfill for traditional students and middle class students. They reminded Treasury that the non-traditional students, who make up the majority at some institutions, tend to have fewer resources and greater family responsibilities. They would have very little room in their busy schedules for a requirement that would not have a positive effect on their job or their performance at school. One respondent suggested that very few would choose the credit over paid work, which would result in "money left on the table." Some students would struggle to get to their community service assignments due to limits in public transportation, and other obligations during normal business hours. For example, students with lab work, or student teaching obligations could only do community service during hours where service is less likely to be needed. Respondents provided several anecdotes about students who work long hours.

Parent/Child Relationship: A few respondents focused on the parent/child relationship and stressed that the obligation to perform the community service falls on students, even though it is the parents receiving the tax benefits. (This is the case when the student is a dependent on the parent's return.) These respondents expressed concern that students might not treat the requirements for receipt of the credit seriously or follow through on their commitments, thus leaving their parents unable to claim the credit. One gave the example of first year students struggling to acclimate to college life who might not "get it together" in time, thus leaving their parents without access to the credit. Another respondent thought that this obligation would create "unnecessary stress" between parents and children as parents work to make sure the service is performed and that their children provide them the necessary documentation. This respondent also suggested that the students' Thirteenth Amendment rights may be violated by a program where the person forced to provide the service (perhaps involuntarily) is likely different from the benefiting taxpayer. In summary, all respondents addressing the parent/child relationship thought that "burdening" parents in this way was unfair. No respondent who commented on the family relationship viewed the joint obligation as appropriate.

D. Conclusion

This section has explored the feasibility of creating a volunteer requirement for receipt of the AOTC. The analysis shows that although it might be possible to implement such a requirement, it could not be done in a manner consistent with good tax policy. The requirement would be expensive to both education institutions and the IRS to administer, would contribute to taxpayer compliance burden, could burden the volunteer sector, and could decrease participation rates in existing tax-based education programs.

XII   Conclusion

Most of the Federal support for individuals pursuing higher education is available through two government agencies: the Department of Education, which is responsible for a number of federally supported direct grants and student loans, and the Department of the Treasury, which is responsible for the tax provisions administered by the Internal Revenue Service. The foundation of the Department of Education's student aid programs is the Pell Grant. Pell Grants are need-based grants to assist individuals from low- and moderate-income households with their undergraduate education expenses. For the 2012 academic year, the maximum Pell grant is $5,550. The main tax benefit for undergraduates is the American Opportunity tax credit (AOTC). The AOTC is a partially refundable credit that provides up to $2,500 in support to families with expenses for tuition and fees earning less than $90,000 ($180,000 for those filing joint returns). The ARRA fully funded an increase in the maximum Pell Grant to $5,550 in 2010, and created the AOTC as a substitute for the Hope credit (and to some extent the lifetime learning credit), which was worth a maximum of $1,800 ($2,000 for the lifetime learning credit).

In 2009, 8.98 million tax returns claimed $15.8 billion in American Opportunity Tax Credits for an average tax credit of about $1,760. In addition, during FY2010 an estimated 8.9 million students received $36.5 billion in Pell Grant Awards for an average award of $4,115.

Although many additional benefits exist to assist families with education expenses, this report focuses on the ARRA and the Pell Grants. This report examines some of the issues surrounding the coordination of these benefits and explores some of the ways that the delivery of these benefits could be improved so that more students could receive the maximum amount of aid to which they were entitled and in a manner that improved their ability to make good decisions about pursuing additional education. The report presents an analysis of the way these two benefits interact, sometimes supplementing each other, but sometimes at least partially offsetting each other. As shown in the report, Pell Grants are targeted at low-income and modest income families; in contrast, tax credits are more effective at targeting benefits to those with positive tax liability. The report also examined the feasibility of adding a volunteer requirement to the AOTC.

The report presents four options for improving the coordination of the benefits:

- *Further simplification of the Pell Grant and the elimination of asset information from the determination of Pell Grant amounts.* This would create simplification without having large effects on the distribution of benefits. The majority of families receiving Pell grants have few major assets outside of their homes and retirement plans, which are already excluded in determining eligibility.

- *Improve the ability of taxpayers to predict future education tax credit eligibility through the creation of calculators on the Department of Education Web site.* The calculators could predict the likely value of any education tax credit for which the individual was eligible. This would increase the accuracy of taxpayer expectations, increase the visibility of the education credits to eligible individuals who may not be applying, and thus, lead individuals to make more informed decisions about enrollment and education financing.

- *Improve information reporting to IRS so that taxpayers and the IRS have an accurate knowledge of eligible expenses.* Accurate filing is challenging to students (and their families) and the IRS because neither receives an accurate set of information about the actual level of expenses which are eligible for a credit, and little guidance is provided on how to file once the accurate level of expenses is determined. Improving the quality of the third party information, first by providing accurate detail on amounts received by schools, and not just amounts billed, and second, by providing expense information about room and board separately from expense information on the credits, would improve compliance by taxpayers wishing to be compliant, and provide IRS with a greater ability to provide effective oversight. Although improved reporting would increase the demands on schools and universities, this burden may be appropriate given the size of the amounts received.

- *Exclude all Pell grants from income for tax purposes, including funds used to pay for room and board.* Including the portion of grant amounts used for room and board is complicated, particularly for low-income taxpayers, because of the interaction of the inclusion with other income-based benefits like the EITC and the AOTC itself. Treatment of all other scholarship income would be unchanged. This proposal would provide simplicity at the cost of foregone revenue.

Treasury examined advance refundability of the education tax credits and concludes that this would be challenging, expensive, and less efficient than direct student aid. The report finds that the limited advantages of advance refundability are outweighed by the disadvantages. The report concludes that direct grant aid, such as the Pell Grant, is a better mechanism for delivering education subsidies to low-income students.

This report also considers the feasibility of a volunteer service requirement embedded in the education tax credit. Such a requirement would be at odds with the general focus on simplification proposed here. As presented in the analysis, a requirement of this nature would not represent good tax policy. Technically, it could be accomplished. However, it is likely that the requirement would be impossible to implement in a way that was fair, consistent with the goals of the credit, and for which reasonable levels of compliance could be maintained.

Appendix: Statutory Language

Section 1004(f) of the American Recovery and Reinvestment Act of 2009, Treasury Studies Regarding Education Incentives:

(1) The Secretary of the Treasury and the Secretary of Education, or their delegates, shall--

(A) study how to coordinate the credit allowed under section 25A of the Internal Revenue Code of 1986 with the Federal Pell Grant program under section 401 of the Higher Education Act of 1965 to maximize their effectiveness at promoting college affordability, and

(B) examine ways to expedite the delivery of the tax credit.

(2) The Secretary of the Treasury and the Secretary of Education, or their delegates, shall study the feasibility of requiring including community service as a condition of taking their tuition and related expenses into account under section 25A of the Internal Revenue Code of 1986.

Bibliography

AmeriCorps, 2010. http://www.americorps.gov/ (last accessed June 10, 2011).

Bettinger, Eric P., Bridget T. Long, Philip Oreopoulos, and Lisa Sanbonmatsu, 2009. "The Role of Simplification and Information in College Decisions: Results from the H&R Block FAFSA Experiment." *NBER Working Paper No. 15361,* National Bureau of Economic Research, Cambridge MA.

Belley, Phillippe and Lance Lochner, 2007. "The Changing Role of Family Income and Ability in Determining Educational Achievement." *Journal of Human Capital*, 1(1), 37-89.

Cameron, Stephen V and Christopher Taber, 2004. "Estimation of Educational Borrowing Constraints Using Returns to Schooling." *Journal of Political Economy Part 1*, 112(2), 132-182.

Campus Compact, 2010. http://www.compact.org/ (last accessed July 29, 2011).

Center for the Study of Education Policy, 2011. *Grapevine, an Annual Compilation of Data on State Fiscal Support for Higher Education.* Illinois State University, Normal IL. http://www.grapevine.ilstu.edu/index.shtml (last accessed June 10, 2011).

College Board, 2010. *Trends in Student Aid 2010.* http://trends.collegeboard.org/student_aid (last accessed June 10, 2011).

Community College League of California, 2004. *Responding to the California Performance Review.* http://www.ccleague.org/files/public/cpr-report.pdf (last accessed June 10, 2011).

Council of Economic Advisors, 2009. *Simplifying Student Aid: The Case for an Easier, Faster and More Accurate FAFSA.* National Economic Council, Council of Economic Advisors, Washington DC.

Dynarski, Susan and Judith Scott-Clayton, 2007. "College Grants on a Postcard: A Proposal for Simple and Predictable Federal Student Aid." *Hamilton Project Discussion Paper.* Washington DC.

Dynarski, Susan and Judith Scott-Clayton, 2006. "The Cost of Complexity in Federal Student Aid: lessons from Optimal Tax Theory and Behavioral Economics." *National Tax Journal*, 59 No. 2. 319-56.

Ellwood, David T. and Thomas J, Kane, 2000. "Securing the Future: Investing in Children from Birth to College" in *Who is Getting a College Education? Family Background and the growing Gaps in Enrollment,* edited by Sheldon Danziger and Jane Waldfogel. Russell Sage Foundation NY, 283-324.

Grantmaker Forum on Community and National Service, 2003. *The Cost of a Volunteer: What it Takes to Provide a Quality Volunteer Experience.* http://www.pacefunders.org/publications/pubs/Cost%20Volunteer%20FINAL.pdf (last accessed June 10, 2011)

Kleven, Henrick, Martin Knudsen, Martin, Claus Kreiner, Soren Pedersen, and Emmanuel Saez, 2010 "Unwilling or Unable to Cheat? Evidence from a Randomized Tax Audit Experiment in Denmark." *NBER Working Paper No. 15769.* National Bureau of Economic Research, Cambridge MA.

Lochner, Lance, and Alexander Monge-Naranjo, 2008. "The Nature of Credit Constraints and Human Capital." *NBER Working Paper No. 13912.* National Bureau of Economic Research, Cambridge MA.

Long, Bridget T., 2006. "College Tuition Pricing and Federal Financial Aid: Is there a Connection?" Testimony before the U.S. Senate Committee on Finance, December 5, 2006.

Mazur, Mark and Alan H. Plumley. 2007. "Understanding the Tax Gap." *National Tax Journal*, 60 No. 3. 569-576.

National Association of College and University Business Officers, 2010. *NACUBO -- Common Fund Study of Endowments (NCSE): Press Release.* http://www.nacubo.org/Documents/research/2009_NCSE_Press_Release.pdf (last accessed June 10, 2011).

National Center for Education Statistics 2012. *Postsecondary Institutions and Price of Attendance in 2011-12, Degrees and Other Awards Conferred: 2010-11, and 12-Month Enrollment: 2010-2011 First Look (Provisional Data), 2012.* NCES No. 2012-289rev. http://nces.ed.gov/pubs2012/2012289rev.pdf (last accessed December 4, 2012).

National Center for Education Statistics, 2011. *Digest of Education Statistics, 2010.* NCES No. 20011015. U.S. Department of Education, Institute of Education Sciences. http://nces.ed.gov/pubsearch/pubsinfo.asp?pubid=2011015 (last accessed June 10, 2011).

National Center for Education Statistics, 2010. *Digest of Education Statistics, 2009.* NCES No. 2010013. U.S. Department of Education, Institute of Education Sciences. http://nces.ed.gov/pubsearch/pubsinfo.asp?pubid=2010013 (last accessed June 10, 2011).

National Center for Education Statistics, 2009. "2007-08 National Postsecondary Student Aid Study (NPSAS:08): Student Financial Aid Estimates for 2007-2008." NCES 2009-166. U.S. Department of Education, Institute of Education Sciences. http://nces.ed.gov/pubs2009/2009166.pdf (last accessed June 11, 2011).

National Service Learning Clearinghouse, 2013. "What is Service-Learning?" http://www.servicelearning.org/what-service-learning. (last accessed June 11, 2013).

Nielsen, Helena, Torben Sorensen and Christopher Taber, 2010. "Estimating the Effect of Student Aid on College Enrollment: Evidence from a Government Grant Policy Reform." *American Economic Journal: Economic Policy*. May 2010, 2(2), 185-215.

Turner, Nicholas, 2010A. "Why Don't Taxpayers Maximize their Tax-Based Student Aid Awards? Salience and Inertia in Program Selection." Paper presented at the 103rd Annual Meeting of the National Tax Association, Chicago, IL.

Turner, Nicholas, 2010B. "Who Benefits From Student Aid? The Economic Incidence of Tax-Based Federal Student Aid." Paper presented at the 102nd Annual Meeting of the National Tax Association, Denver, CO.

U.S. Department of Education, 2012. *Title IV Program Volume Reports.* http://studentaid.ed.gov/about/data-center/student/title-iv (last accessed December 4, 2012).

U.S. Department of Education, 2011. *Description of Federal Pell Grant Program.* http://www2.ed.gov/programs/fpg/index.html (last accessed June 7, 2011)

U.S. Department of Education, 2011. *Description of Federal Work-Study Program (FWS).* http://www2.ed.gov/programs/fws/index.html. (last accessed October 13, 2010).

U.S. Department of Education, 2011. "FY 2012 Department of Education Justifications of Appropriation Estimates to the Congress: Student Financial Assistance" in *President's FY2012 Budget Request for the U.S. Department of Education.* http://www2.ed.gov/about/overview/budget/budget12/justifications/p-sfa.pdf (last accessed June 9, 2011).

U.S. Department of Education, 2010. *2008-2009 Federal Pell Grant Program End of Year Report.* http://www2.ed.gov/finaid/prof/resources/data/pell-2008-09/pell-eoy-08-09.pdf (last accessed June 11, 2011)

U.S. Department of Education, 2009. *Report to Congress on Efforts to Simplify the Free Application for Federal Student Aid (FAFSA)* http://www2.ed.gov/policy/highered/leg/hea08/fafsa-report.pdf (last accessed June 7, 2011).

U.S. Department of the Treasury, 2013. "General Explanations of the Administration's Fiscal Year 2014 Revenue Proposals." http://www.treasury.gov/resource-center/tax-policy/Documents/General-Explanations-FY2014.pdf (last accessed May 13, 2013).

U.S. Department of the Treasury, 2010. "Feasibility of Including a Volunteer Requirement for Receipt of Federal Education Tax Credits." Federal Register Doc No. 2010-7021. *Federal Register,* 75(60), 15772.

U.S. Department of the Treasury. Internal Revenue Service, 2012. "IRS Releases New Tax Gap Estimates; Compliance Rates Remain Statistically Unchanged From Previous Study." Press release. Washington, D.C., January 6, 2012. http://www.irs.gov/newsroom/article/0,,id=252038,00.html

U.S. Department of the Treasury. Internal Revenue Service, 2010. *Exemptions, Standard Deductions and Filing Information for use in preparing 2010 Returns.* IRS publication 501. http://www.irs.gov/pub/irs-pdf/p501.pdf. Washington DC.

U.S. Department of the Treasury. Internal Revenue Service, 1999. "Advance Earned Income Tax Credit: 1994 and 1997 Notice Study: A Report to Congress." August 1999. Internal Revenue Service, Washington DC.

U.S. Department of the Treasury. Internal Revenue Service, 1996. "Federal Tax Compliance Research: Individual Income Tax Gap Estimates for 1985, 1988, and 1992." Publication 1415 (rev. 4–96). Washington, D.C., 1996.

U.S. General Accountability Office, 2009. "Federal Student Aid: Highlights of a Study Group on Simplifying the Free Application for Federal Student Aid." GAO-10-29. General Accountability Office, Washington DC.

U.S. General Accountability Office, 2007. "Advance Earned Income Tax Credit: Low Use and Small Dollars Paid Impede IRS's Efforts to Reduce High Noncompliance, Report to the Joint Committee on Taxation." GAO-07-1110. General Accountability Office, Washington DC.

U.S. General Accountability Office, 2004. "Health Coverage Tax Credit: Simplified and More Timely Enrollment Process Could Increase Participation." GAO-04-1029. General Accountability Office, Washington DC.

U.S. General Accountability Office, 2002. "Student Aid and Tax Benefits: Better Research and Guidance Will Facilitate Comparison of Effectiveness and Student Use." GAO-02-751. General Accountability Office, Washington DC.

U. S. Office of Management and Budget, 2011. *Analytical Perspectives, Budget of the United States Government, Fiscal Year 2012.* U.S. Government Printing Office, Washington DC.

White House, 2011. *A Call to Action on College Completion.* Middle Class Task Force Blog, March 23, 2011. http://www.whitehouse.gov/blog/2011/03/23/call-action-college-completion (last accessed July 29, 2011).

White House, 2010. *The American Opportunity Tax Credit and the President's Event Today.* Middle Class Task Force Blog, Oct 13, 2010. http://www.whitehouse.gov/blog/2010/10/13/american-opportunity-tax-credit-and-presidents-event-today (last accessed July 29, 2011).

www.ingramcontent.com/pod-product-compliance
Lightning Source LLC
Chambersburg PA
CBHW052005280526
45793CB00005B/856